The Complete
Book of
Drawing
Nature

The Complete Book of
Drawing Nature

BARRINGTON BARBER

ARCTURUS

ARCTURUS

This edition published in 2021 by Arcturus Publishing Limited
26/27 Bickels Yard, 151–153 Bermondsey Street,
London SE1 3HA

Copyright © Arcturus Holdings Limited/Barrington Barber

ISBN: 978-1-83857-427-7
AD006650UK

Printed in China

CONTENTS

Introduction

There is enough to draw in the natural world to keep you busy for the rest of your life. Nature is easy enough to find, wherever you are, because even in the centre of a city, you can usually see the sky or find some form of vegetation. Even a small suburban garden can hugely increase your store of knowledge about nature.

The world of plants, upon which both humans and animals rely so greatly for their existence, constitutes a vast area of work for the artist, which might be said to culminate in the execution of an entire landscape. However, before you get around to landscapes, you must first take a good hard look at a range of plants and flowers, in order to understand the rules of growth patterns and how they are repeated. Once you have observed these at close quarters, it is much easier to draw the plants so they actually look as though they are growing. In the first chapter of this book we shall start by focusing on plants, flowers and small areas of vegetation, honing your observation skills and your drawing technique.

Another aspect of nature drawing that you can practise without leaving the comfort of your own home is still life, which is the focus of the second chapter in this book. For centuries, artists have been studying the forms of fruit, flowers, stones, shells and other natural objects, and arranging them into pleasing compositions.

Returning to the outside world, we shall look at the many wonderful shapes and seasonal displays of trees and how you can render them convincingly. Some elements of the natural world are difficult to draw and you will have to study them over and over again in order to understand how they could work as drawings. One example is the element of water, which produces myriad visual effects for you to try to capture. We shall be looking in depth at how to draw stones, rock formations and water in its various guises, as well as the sky, sun and clouds.

In the final two chapters of the book, we shall focus on drawing landscapes, from exploring a location and choosing a viewpoint for your own drawing, to studying the compositions of master artists. Producing landscapes, in any medium, is an excellent pursuit. Apart from getting you out into the world and helping you to appreciate its beauties and structure, it calms the mind and soothes the emotions. As you draw and observe, observe and draw, a certain detached acceptance of what is there in front of you takes over. It is also fascinating to discover ways of translating impressions of an outside scene into a two-dimensional set of marks on paper. Whether or not you share some of your experience of your observation with others, it is a truly beneficial activity.

Drawing Materials

The first thing to consider before you start drawing is your choice of materials. There are many possibilities and good specialist art shops will be able to supply you with all sorts of materials and advice. However, here are some of the basics to start with.

Pencils, graphite and charcoal

Good pencils are an absolute necessity, and you will need several grades of blackness or softness. You will find a B (soft) pencil to be your basic drawing instrument, and I would suggest a 2B, 4B, and a 6B for all your normal drawing requirements. Then a propelling or clutch pencil will be useful for any fine drawing that you do, because the lead maintains a consistently thin line. A 0.5mm or 0.3mm does very well.

Another useful tool is a graphite stick, which is a thick length of graphite that can be sharpened to a point. The edge of the point can also be used for making thicker, more textured, marks.

An historic drawing medium is, of course, charcoal, which is basically a length of carbonized willow twig. This will give you marvellous smoky texture, as well as dark heavy lines and thin grey ones. It is also very easy to smudge, which helps you to produce areas of tone quickly.

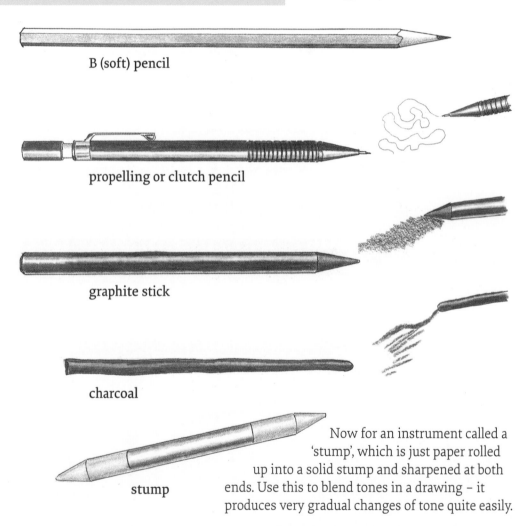

B (soft) pencil

propelling or clutch pencil

graphite stick

charcoal

stump

Now for an instrument called a 'stump', which is just paper rolled up into a solid stump and sharpened at both ends. Use this to blend tones in a drawing – it produces very gradual changes of tone quite easily.

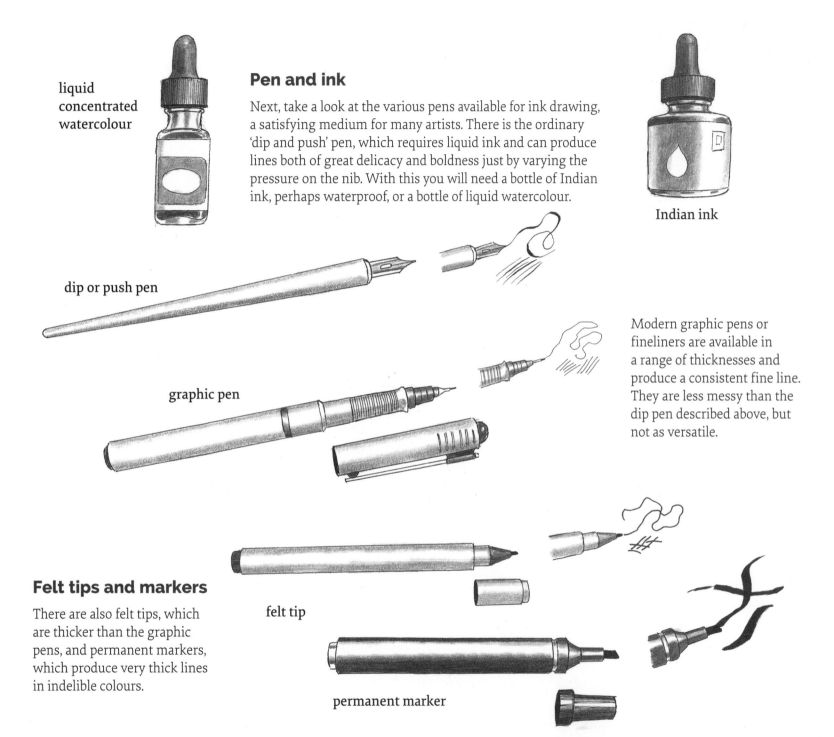

liquid
concentrated
watercolour

Pen and ink

Next, take a look at the various pens available for ink drawing, a satisfying medium for many artists. There is the ordinary 'dip and push' pen, which requires liquid ink and can produce lines both of great delicacy and boldness just by varying the pressure on the nib. With this you will need a bottle of Indian ink, perhaps waterproof, or a bottle of liquid watercolour.

Indian ink

dip or push pen

Modern graphic pens or fineliners are available in a range of thicknesses and produce a consistent fine line. They are less messy than the dip pen described above, but not as versatile.

graphic pen

Felt tips and markers

There are also felt tips, which are thicker than the graphic pens, and permanent markers, which produce very thick lines in indelible colours.

felt tip

permanent marker

Brushes

If you wish to work in brush and wash, you will need
a couple of brushes of different thicknesses; I find that
Nos 2 and 8 are the most useful. The best brushes are
sable hair, but some nylon brushes are quite adequate.
Use your brushes with a liquid watercolour as shown
on page 9.

No.2 sable or nylon brush

No.8 sable or nylon brush

craft knife

scalpel

Erasers

When using pencil you will almost certainly want to get rid of
some of the lines you have drawn. There are many types of eraser,
but a good solid one (of rubber or plastic) and a kneadable eraser
(known as a 'putty rubber') are both worth having. The putty
rubber is a very efficient tool, useful for very black drawings; used
with a dabbing motion, it lifts and removes marks leaving no
residue on the paper.

soft rubber eraser

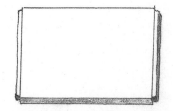

putty or kneadable eraser

Sharpeners

Don't forget you will need some way of sharpening
your pencils frequently, so investing in a good
pencil-sharpener, either manual or electric, is well
worth it. Many artists prefer keeping their pencils
sharp with a craft knife or a scalpel. Of the two, a
craft knife is safer, although a scalpel is sharper.

Working in Colour

Throughout this book I have shown examples drawn in colour and, as you will see, colour can add an extra dimension to your work. If you enjoy working in colour, experiment with some of the options shown here.

Felt tip pens and illuminators

These pens allow thicker, more solid areas of colour to be put on quickly and are useful for larger drawings.

Coloured pencils

Don't concern yourself too much with the brand, although some are better than others. Go for as many variations in colour as you can find. Thinner pencils can be of superior quality but that is not always the case. Try them out and make your own judgement. Watercolour pencils are similar to ordinary coloured pencils but you can use a brush with water to spread their colour over larger areas, so they work well for landscapes. There are several brands available.

Fineline graphic pens

These pens are good for drawing and behave similarly to a coloured pencil but with a more intense colour value.

Soft pastels

These come in a wide range of colours and are very useful if you want to spread or smudge your marks. However, they are very expensive and tend to get used up quickly.

Hard pastels

Also known as conté crayons, these are essentially the same material as the soft ones but bound together in a compressed form. They are square in section whereas the soft ones are round. Hard pastels last longer and are easier to manipulate. The range of colours is again enormous.

Liquid watercolour (concentrated)

These colours are just like ink but may be diluted with water. They can be used with a pen or a brush.

Watercolour box

Watercolours are easiest to use from a box, especially if you are working outdoors, but they can be bought in small tubes as well.

Warm-up Exercises

To get started, let's look at some patterns that have their origin in nature. These are all doodles, but they are representative of what you might see growing in the countryside or in your garden.

For the first shape, make a small circle with five small lines coming out from it, then draw petal shapes around the outside of the lines. The result looks like a flower.

The next one is similar in design, but the petals are more pointed and there are six of them this time.

Draw a small circle then put elongated petals around it, one at the top, one opposite at the bottom and one either side to form a cross. Fill in with four diagonal petals. In the spaces between, draw partially visible petals, followed by an outer set.

To draw a Tudor rose, start again with a circle, then put in five sets of small lines radiating from it. Around this, draw a five-petalled rose shape with overlapping edges, then put a small leaf shape projecting from the edge of each petal. Then draw in the last set of petal shapes in between each leaf.

The last flower shape is a bit like a chrysanthemum, with multiple long, thin, pointed petals radiating from a central point.

Next we go on to plant-like shapes with a central stalk. These drawings will help you to get a feel for the way in which natural growth proceeds. The first is just a straight stalk with a leaf shape on the end and additional stalks growing out of the central one, each bearing a leaf. Make the middle leaves larger and the bottom leaves smaller.

In the next drawing there is again a straight stalk, but the branches are all curling. Keep the twigs at the top and bottom simple and allow the middle layers to be more complex. Notice how some curl one way and some the other. Play around and experiment.

Here the stalk is drawn more substantially, thickest at the base and tapering to a point at the top. Draw the lower branches also with a bit of thickness and allow small, straight twigs to branch off in all directions. Try to maintain the same growth pattern all over the plant.

The last drawing is a similar growth pattern, but this time all the branches and twigs are curly. Start with the central trunk and add the thicker branches first before putting in the smaller ones. Have fun and be inventive.

Here we look at developing a feel for the different textures you will find in the natural world and how you can use your drawing materials to capture them.

Leaves

All that is needed to give the effect of thick, hedge-like leaves is a large number of small leaves drawn adjacent to and overlapping each other. Try to maintain a certain amount of variety in the angles of the leaves to make them more convincing.

Grass

The first of these drawings of texture shows an impression of an area of grass-like tufts – that is to say, very conventional patterns that resemble grass, not drawings taken directly from life. When you have tried the stylized version, you could go and look at a real lawn and try to draw that from life.

Wood

Now try doing this wooden plank, with its knots and wavy lines of growth. The floorboards in your house might be a good example of this kind of wood pattern.

Water

This watery texture is achieved by keeping all the marks you make horizontal and joined together to create the effect of ripples. Smudge a little of the drawing to create greyer tones, but leave some untouched areas to look like reflected light.

Beach

Next, a drawing that resembles a pebbled beach, with countless stones of various sizes.

Rock

This drawing shows the surface of what might be a piece of grained and fissured rock.

Fur

This resembles fur, such as on a rug or the back of a cat. The short, wavy lines go in several directions, but follow a sort of pattern.

Clouds

This smoky texture is produced by using a soft pencil, then a paper stump to smudge the dark areas. After that, a little rubbing of some of the darker parts gives a cloudy look.

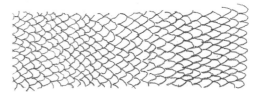

Snakeskin

Drawing snakeskin or fish scales is just a matter of drawing many overlapping scale shapes without being too precise or you will lose the movable look of natural scales.

Chapter One

FLOWERS AND PLANTS

Plants are very accommodating subject matter when you are learning to draw. They don't move about a lot; they remain the same shape while you are drawing them; a great many of them you can bring indoors to observe at your convenience; and they offer an enormous variety of shapes, structures and textures. Even if you are keen to get started on a landscape, drawing plants and flowers is a valuable first step and never a waste of time. What you learn from observing and rendering their growth patterns will stand you in good stead when you start on drawing a tree, or a full-blown landscape.

The essential structure of a plant is not difficult to see if you study it for a time. Take a group of leaved plants: you will soon notice how one type will have leaves in clusters that spring up at the points of the stems, whereas in another the leaves will hang down around a central point. Some plants have stalks coming off the branches evenly at the same point, others have the stalks staggered alternately down the length of the stem. Once you are familiar with a plant's characteristic shape and appearance, you will begin to notice similar properties in other plants.

When it comes to drawing a plant in bloom, note the fragility of the flower and the shapes of its petals. Observe the texture and structure of the petals and stamens and how carefully you need to trace your line. Don't use heavy lines, because the effect they produce will contradict the delicacy of the flower.

After looking at outdoor and indoor plants, single flowers and flowers in groups, we shall finish the chapter by studying the effects of wider areas of vegetation and how they can be shown in a small scene.

Simple Leaf Shapes

Starting with some simple examples will give you confidence in your ability to draw plant material. Try sketching various leaf shapes, to sharpen your eye as to how plants look. Observe whether the leaf edges are serrated or smooth, and how the veins curve out from the central stem; if the edge of the leaf is curling up as the leaf dries, draw the curling shapes exactly as you see them.

Adding tone

Collect a few leaves from your garden or local park and take them inside to study their shapes and textures in more detail.

Notice how you can concentrate on a small object such as this with great precision, showing how the veins of the leaf shape the outer form and how, as the leaf starts to dry out and decay, the edges curl up and form interesting shapes. When you try this out, give every detail your attention and treat the leaf as seriously as you would a large, complex object. Shade carefully with your pencil, leaving fine lines unshaded to denote the leaf veins, and applying extra pressure to create the darkest areas of shadow. Draw the shadow beneath the leaf as well and see how your dedication makes the small leaf become a really powerful image.

Flowers

Now go a step further. Select some flowers that you find attractive – you will give them more attention if you like the look of them – and then proceed to draw one or two blooms with the same sort of detailed attention that you gave to drawing the leaves. You will need to be a little more delicate in the way you approach them because they are much more fragile and exquisite than the leaves, which have a rough vigour.

Here is a rose, with its inner petals tightly folded around the centre of the flower. The edges of the petals need to be drawn with a certain amount of sensitivity to get the feel of their texture.

Next I tried a couple of pansies, one facing towards me and one turning away, so that I could get some idea of the shape of the flower from different angles. As you can see, I have sketched in some leaves – but at this stage the shape of the whole plant doesn't matter so much.

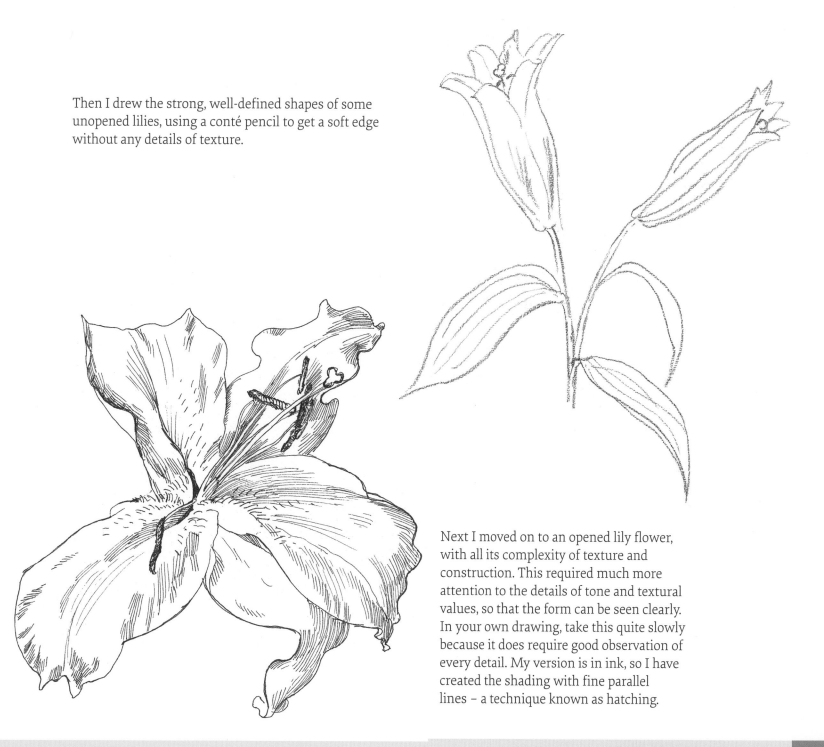

Then I drew the strong, well-defined shapes of some unopened lilies, using a conté pencil to get a soft edge without any details of texture.

Next I moved on to an opened lily flower, with all its complexity of texture and construction. This required much more attention to the details of tone and textural values, so that the form can be seen clearly. In your own drawing, take this quite slowly because it does require good observation of every detail. My version is in ink, so I have created the shading with fine parallel lines – a technique known as hatching.

Houseplants

When it comes to drawing a larger plant such as this houseplant, the important thing is not to try to draw everything exactly, but to convey a feeling of growth and of the overall structure. Avoid using heavy lines, especially when you start your drawing.

First of all, sketch the main structure of the plant, indicating the way its stems splay out and, in the case of the example I've chosen, the way that the long leaves fan outwards. Try to draw the initial line of the stems in one smooth go, to give yourself a better 'feel' of the way that the plant grows.

Having drawn the plant's main outline, the next stage is to express the floating, flexible quality of the long leaves. Some will appear stronger and darker in tone, while others will be far less distinct. Try capturing the character of these leaves by the way that you draw them. It does not matter too much if, when you look back at the plant, they seem to have altered. Total accuracy is not essential here.

With this basil plant, the trick is not to overdraw the darker areas. One or two of the leaves at the back and bottom of the plant will be in deep shade, but most of them will be relatively light in tone. Again, it doesn't matter if some of your leaves are not exactly in the right place, as long as they look fairly natural relative to the other leaves.

Artist's Tip

Once you start drawing larger plants, you realize that drawing every leaf is very time consuming. Some artists do just this, but most devise a way of repeating the typical leaf shape of the plant and then draw in the leaves quickly in characteristic groups. It is not necessary to count all the leaves and render them precisely, just put in enough to make your drawing convincing.

A Flowering Plant in Colour

This drawing in coloured pencils shows a potted plant with pink blossoms and light green leaves. When using coloured pencils you will need to work fairly thoroughly over the areas of colour, as pencils do not produce very strong colours, unlike paint.

Step 1

To start with, draw an outline of the flowers and pot, in a pinkish colour similar to the flowers. At this stage no detail is necessary, but the outline should be as clear and accurate as possible.

Step 2

In the next stage, you can put in the main colours with a reasonable amount of solidity. Choose your colours carefully to match what you see, and if you don't have exactly the right colour, combine two colours. For the shadowed foliage in the middle of the plant, I drew in a base layer of green before adding brown over the top. For white flowers, leave the paper showing through as I have done.

Step 3

The next step is really the main part, where you must work up the darkest tones and deepest colours to get an effect of the dimensions and contrast between the parts in shade and the brightest areas. Don't forget a little shading on the pot and a light shadow cast on the table. You may also wish to add a simple background colour to complete your drawing.

Plants and Flowers: Detailed Study

Before you begin to draw, look at the plant closely: at the bloom (if there is one), and note how the leaves grow out of the stalk. Look at it from above, to see the leaves radiating out from the centre; and from the side, to see the different appearance of the leaf shapes as they project towards you, away from you and to each side as they spiral round the stem. Note the texture of the leaves, and how it compares with that of other plants.

The sedum has a beautiful spiralling arrangement of leaves that curves up into a dish-like form. Rain must fill up the hollow of the leaf and run down the stalk to water the plant's roots.

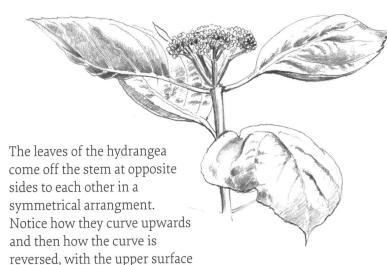

The appearance of the tulip is very formal and upright, with its closed cup-like flower and long stiff stalk and leaves.

The leaves of the hydrangea come off the stem at opposite sides to each other in a symmetrical arrangment. Notice how they curve upwards and then how the curve is reversed, with the upper surface bulging out towards the tip.

The delicate bloom of the camellia looks so fragile. It contrasts beautifully with the solid, perfect shape of the leaves.

Here we have two blooms from the same plant (a clematis) at different stages of its growth. The difference is quite dramatic.

The clematis captured as it is just opening, with its smooth-looking petals hanging down.

The fully open bloom, centre showing to the sun. By this stage the edges of the petals are quite crinkly.

Growth Patterns

Nature offers so much variety, as you will discover once you start studying it in earnest. In the plants shown on this spread you will find three very different effects in as many examples.

Compare them, and note the differences you observe. You will find these patterns of growth fascinating as you investigate them more fully and extend your experience.

The blossom of the cherry tree clings closely to the dark, stiff, almost spiky branches.

The habit of the stewartia is to gracefully hold its leaves and small blooms away from the main branch.

The acorns and leaves of the oak
jut out from their stalk.

Step-by-Step Practice

Plants are living organisms, and you'll notice if you draw for any length of time that you can observe their gentle movement. When you tackle them you'll need to study them for a few minutes before you start, in order to see their structure. Approach them rather as a botanist might, being clear in your own mind as to the shape of what you're going to draw.

Step 1

The first thing is to draw the basic cup shape of these tulip flowers, standing erect on their stems. A couple of leaves growing off the stem helps to add to the picture.

Step 2

Then, without drawing too heavily, put in the tonal values, so that the light can be seen coming through the petals. When you try this drawing, don't overdo the tone or the tulips will start to look too solid and heavy. As the colour on the petals is in fine striations it's a good idea to draw your tonal lines in the same direction as the colour.

Step 1

These flowers, drawn in coloured pastel, are from a japonica bush. The branches of this bush are quite rigid and solid and the flowers seem to grow almost directly off them, juxtaposing strength and delicacy. The first thing is to map out the positions of the blooms on the branches. Only a few are drawn here, but it's not difficult to draw many more as long as you observe the pattern of the growth.

Step 2

Once again, observe the way that the petals are formed and draw the tonal areas in the direction of the growth of the petal. I used varied pink tones for the petals, overlaid with white to indicate the light falling on the plant. A few additions in dark blue and purple help to define the outer edges of the petals and the branches.

Draw a Rose in Steps

In this drawing I have included a dark background behind the single rose. This has the effect of throwing the flower into relief and giving the drawing a more dramatic feel.

Step 1

Draw a rough shape to indicate the main form of the flower and its leaves.

Step 3

Put a light tone over the whole composition except where you can see there are highlights.

Step 2

Next, describe more carefully the exact shapes of the petals and leaves.

Step 4

Block in the dark tones behind the flower and add the more linear dark tone on the petals, stem and leaves.

Step 5

Now blend all the areas of tone to finish your drawing. If the highlights have smudged, use an eraser to pick them out again. The result of your hard work will be a lively and interesting portrayal of a rose.

Vegetation

When you come to draw larger areas of plants, you will need to reduce the amount of detail in order to convey the overall impression of growth in a naturalistic manner. Here, the aim is to portray plants and flowers as they might appear in a wider view of a garden or landscape. Study these examples and find similar ones to draw yourself.

The first example I have chosen (right) is the remarkable *Large Tuft of Grass* after Albrecht Durer (1471–1528). Since the view here is in close proximity to the vegetation, the artist is obliged to differentiate between the thin stalks of cultivated grass and the wider-leaved versions that grow in fields and meadows. This is not grass from a croquet lawn or bowling green, but a coarser, wild version.

This view of a herbaceous border, seen from the height of the tallest flowers, gives a very good idea of the variety of blooms that can be gathered in one spot. The larger flowers are clearly outlined, especially those closest to us, and this contrasts with the more impressionistic aspect of the flowers situated further back. The general idea is to produce enough texture by drawing the tops of each plant and thereby avoid having to build up any darker tones to create depth.

In this example we have leaves simply outlined in ink, using three colours. Observe how leaves grow in clusters and bunches, so that you begin to see the patterns they make.

The fig tree provides a good example of massed leaf forms that give a general idea of how vegetation can look as part of a larger landscape.

This corner of an overgrown garden is a good example of a study of plant life. When you come to draw a landscape these details may not be the focus of your composition, but if you don't get them right the overall picture will suffer. One exercise you should engage in is to make several attempts at just drawing plants in all their profusion – the more wild and tangled, the better.

This view of a valley with a tower and other buildings is seen past the profusion of wild plants on the side of the hillside nearest to our viewpoint. The nearer plants are drawn more heavily in outline than the buildings in the background, which helps to bring the foreground plants forward and push the buildings back.

This edge of a countryside path has the usual mix of wild plants growing along it – a good test of your drawing ability, even if they never end up in a complete landscape.

A Floral Border in Watercolour

In this exercise we look at how you might use watercolours to paint the mass of vegetation and flowers in a floral border. I have chosen to focus on a length of border of just a few metres, ignoring any further background to the scene.

Step 2

The next step is to begin to show the main shapes and colours of the flowers, stalks and leaves. This is all done with simple splodges of watercolour paint, and light strokes of paint for the taller stalks. Try to make your marks as simple as possible, while still showing the main shapes of the flowers concerned. At this stage a lot of white space is still seen around the marks made on the paper, with the exception of the grass in the foreground, which has been put in with a simple light wash of green. To keep your colours fresh, wash your brush thoroughly each time you change colour.

Step 1

At first I have just indicated the outlying colour marks that will define the extent of my picture. I used a fine watercolour brush to make small marks, showing the main colours of green, pink, yellow, blue and purple. The green denotes the edge of the grass in a broken line along the front of the border.

Step 3

Wait for your watercolour to dry, then put in the rest of the greenish background tones of the leaves and stalks. This tonal leafy mass can be done in a variety of greens, some yellower and some darker and bluer. You can also add the deeper colours of the flowers, taking care to show their outside edge against the green background. This can be quite fiddly, but it is necessary to get a good result. Finally, extend and deepen your green wash for the lawn in front of the border.

Chapter Two

NATURE
STILL LIFES

You might think of nature drawing as an outdoor pursuit, but in fact there are many natural objects around your home that you can study and make into satisfying arrangements. From fruit, vegetables and flowers to stones and shells, natural objects have always been central to still-life compositions.

In this chapter we'll begin by drawing single objects, focusing on shape, surface texture and the way light falls over the object. The ability to differentiate between textures in one picture and to give a sense of the feel of the objects you draw is a skill that you must develop if you want to produce good still lifes.

When it comes to making still-life arrangements, keep them fairly simple and straightforward to start with. Don't spread your objects out too much. Concentrate on seeing how a series of overlapping shapes can build a different overall shape. One of the best methods of learning about still-life composition is to look at the work of other artists to understand approaches that might work for you. We'll see examples after master artists in the still-life genre such as Henri Fantin-Latour (1836–1904) and Paul Cézanne (1839–1906).

A Single Apple

With any still life in the home, your fruit bowl is a good place to begin. Start by taking a single apple and studying it.

Begin by carefully drawing in the basic spherical outline of the apple, along with the short stalk coming out of the hollow at the top.

The apple needs to be shaded in a vertical direction between the upper surface and the bottom, concentrating on the left-hand side to indicate the direction of light. Don't forget to add a cast shadow on the surface where the apple is resting: this will add a sense of dimension to your drawing.

Identifying the source of light

The type of shadow that an object throws varies depending on the direction of the source of light. A simple way of learning about shadows is to arrange an object at various angles and note the differences. A lamp is an ideal source of light for this exercise, enabling you to experiment and produce a variety of shadows. Here, notice how the apple with the light full on it and the apple silhouetted against the light look less three-dimensional than the apples lit side-on.

A Pine Cone in Steps

Take another, more complex natural object like this pine cone, and draw it as accurately as you can. As with the plants in the previous chapter, the key is to observe the pattern of growth. The strong contrast between the dark inside edges and the lighter outside ones creates a very well-defined set of shapes that should be a pleasure to draw.

Step 1

Draw in the main shape loosely, gaining an idea of the angles of the pine cone's sections.

Step 3

Put in the areas of shade lightly, all over the darker parts of the cone. The highlighted areas are at the ends of the scales.

Step 2

Define it next with a careful outline of all the parts, showing the blocky shapes of the opened scales of the cone.

Step 4

Mark in the darkest parts, noting how the deeper hollows in the cone look much darker.

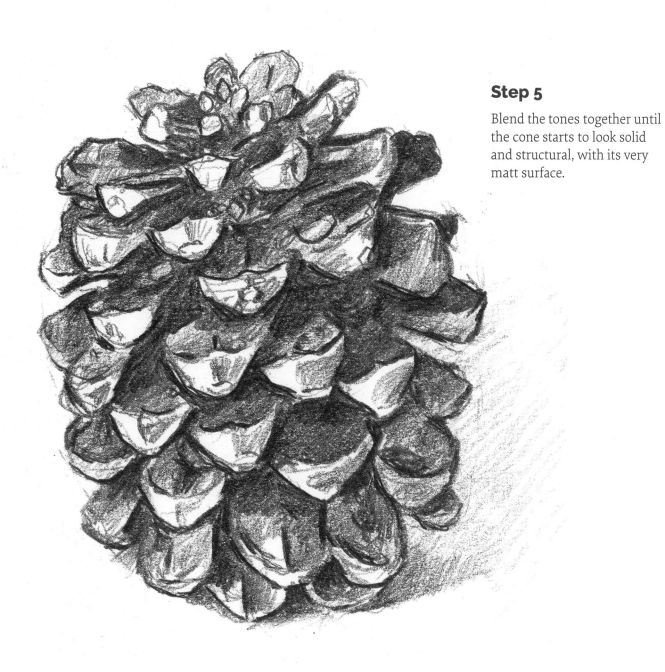

Step 5

Blend the tones together until the cone starts to look solid and structural, with its very matt surface.

Grouping Objects

Now we're going to move on to groups of objects – always trickier than single items as you have to consider their relationship to each other.

Start with an orange and lemon, placing them in such a way that one overlaps the other. This means that you have to consider the size of one compared with the other, as well as the different shapes. When you put in the tone, notice how the shading on the lower part of the orange helps to show up the shape of the lemon.

Now try three objects – two apples and a pear. The space between the apples is very narrow and causes a nice tension between their shapes. The front apple overlaps the pear and helps to contrast the two shapes. Here you are thinking in terms of a still-life composition.

Next we look at the very delicate natural shapes of three seashells. One is showing its hollow, while the next is seen from the reverse side, which helps to create a more interesting contrast. The third is of a different type, which adds more complexity to the arrangement.

Draw a Group of Stones

Natural materials such as rock offer a host of opportunities in terms of their surface. All of the stones in this group are hard, solid objects, but each is at a different stage of weathering. The chunky piece of rock at the top of my collection is not yet eroded to the texture of the two pebbles on the right, which have virtually been worn smooth by the action of water and other pebbles. Find some pebbles or pieces of rock of various sizes and have a go at drawing your own composition.

Step 2

Now draw everything as accurately as you can, describing the irregular facets on some of the stones. Notice the hand-cut transparent piece in the foreground, which is a naturally occurring mineral carved from a larger stone.

Step 1

As usual, draw the first marks very lightly, just to indicate the various sizes and shapes of the objects. Don't get into too much detail yet – just notice the main differences of the stones.

Step 3

Then put in the main areas of tone so that you can begin to see the roundness or angularity of the pieces of stone. Keep the tone very light as yet.

Step 4

Mark in the very darkest tones – as you can see, there aren't very many of these. Most of them are where the stones meet the surface that they are lying on.

Step 5

Now comes the final stage, where you need to be as careful as possible to show how each stone differs from the others. Take your time over this – you won't regret it, as getting the subtleties of each mineral texture is quite an interesting effort to make.

Fruit and Vegetable Textures

Fruit and vegetables are great standbys for natural still lifes, and here we show some examples of how varied they can be in shape and texture.

The bowl of tomatoes gives an idea of the smooth shiny surface of the fruit, and the main aim is to balance the dark and light tones to give a convincing impression of the curved surface.

The cauliflower is an altogether different proposition, having strongly veined leaves and a creamy, lumpy 'curd'. The surface of the vegetable is nowhere smooth and you need to capture the contrast between the dark leaves and the white flowers.

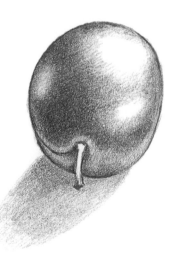

To capture the silky-smooth skin of a plum you need an even application of tone, and obvious highlights to denote the reflective quality of the surface.

These purple grapes are painted smoothly round with most of the colour towards the edges of the fruit and, occasionally, across more of the surface. On each grape, one small area of white paper is left completely untouched to give the effect of the tiny highlight that occurs on glossy objects like grapes. By contrast, the edges can be darkened as much as you like and any spaces between the grapes can be filled in very dark indeed. A bit of background tone, in this case a light watercolour wash, will help to 'anchor' the grapes in place.

The orange requires a stippled or dotted effect to imitate the crinkly nature of the peel.

The generous appearance of these large cabbages provides a very decorative effect, with all the outlines clearly drawn and the vein structure and tonal areas put in with carefully graded lines that follow the contours of the leaves. This is the proper way to build up a strong group of textures that produce an almost tangible sense of the plants' large, fleshy foliage.

Fruit Still Life in Pencil

First collect a few pieces of fruit that appeal to you and arrange them on a surface so that some of them are behind others. I've chosen a bunch of grapes, which I've placed further back than the rest of the fruit, and three tomatoes, an apple and a nectarine.

Step 1

Start off by making a very loose sketch to get some idea as to how the arrangement looks. This drawing is not precise and is really to give you a basis on which to start drawing more definitely.

Step 2

In the next stage, draw the shapes of each piece of fruit quite concisely, making sure that each is as accurate as possible. This is the time to do any correcting and erasing, with the hope that it won't then be necessary in any later stages.

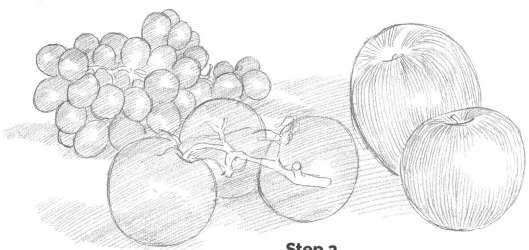

Step 3

Then carefully put in the areas of tone, all in a uniformly light tone. With the larger pieces of fruit, draw the tonal area with your pencil strokes following the form of the fruit.

Step 4

Now all that is needed is to work over all the tonal areas until the darkest to lightest values make sense. One way to see how correct your tonal values are is to half-close your eyes when you look at the still life, which will help you to see tone rather than colour. If you have taken the tone over the highlighted areas by mistake, you can bring those back by using an eraser to re-establish them.

Fruit Still Life in Coloured Pencil

Here I show a wooden bowl with three pears in it, which is lit slightly from behind and from the left. To keep it simple, I have not included any cast shadow in this example, nor any background features at all.

Step 1

The first stage is to draw out the image in one colour. I have chosen a yellow ochre which is not too strong for the yellow pears or the well-lit wooden bowl. Take your time to get the ellipse shape of the bowl correct and don't be afraid to erase and redraw until it looks right. Once you have got the shape of the bowl and the outline of the pears, put in the basic shadow, also in the ochre. Where there are areas of bright highlight, leave the paper showing through.

Step 2

When that is complete, put in yellow over the pears except for the highlights. Then add a warm reddish brown for the deeper tones and colour, followed by green, particularly for the fruit. The shadows on the bowl will also need a touch of green. The method of shading should be with short strokes in many directions. The last colours you will use are blue for the deeper shadows, particularly on the bowl, and black to define some of the edges and where the shadow is really deep.

Fruit Still Life in Pastel

The next picture – in coloured pastels – is also of a bowl of fruit, apples and bananas in a large, painted earthenware bowl. So you will need a range of pastels and a good medium-toned brown or grey paper. Sugar paper or Ingres paper is best for this.

Step 1

The first stage requires a fairly loose brown line drawing on the grey-brown paper and then filling in some of the more obvious shadow areas, including, this time, the cast shadow on the table. Keep the strokes loose and light in touch.

Step 2

You can now begin on the other colours. I put in the blue edge to the bowl and then the basic yellow of the bananas and the yellow and green of the apples. Next, I drew the pattern on the plate and also the very light areas on it. I then deepened the shadows on the bananas and apples with blue and green. The red strokes and touches of highlights were added to the apples. Next, using purple, I put in all the darker shadows in the bowl around the fruit, and also the cast shadow. Lastly, I put in a light green for the tablecloth in the background, with some darker green over the cast shadow. With a looser style than the coloured pencil drawing on pages 52–3, this was much quicker to complete and quite strong and effective.

Flowers: Different Approaches

One of the most popular themes of all time in still-life pictures has been depictions of flowers in vases. The simple, delicate beauty of the blooms, combined with an attractive container, can be handled in so many ways to convey their growth and fragrance. Here I show two very different approaches that you can try out.

Here is a vase of flowers on a windowsill, where you can see the perspective of the surface that it is standing on, the way the light from outside illuminates the objects, and the background of the garden through the window pane. This still-life subject was just waiting to be found and did not require any arrangement prior to drawing. This is one of the benefits of drawing still life – you begin to see your subjects everywhere you look.

Step 1

By contrast, I arranged this glass vase with a stalk of flowers quite carefully before I drew it. As a subject it is both simple and complex, because while there is only one flower and one vase, the latter is glass, which can be difficult to draw convincingly, and the flower is a composite stalk of many small blossoms. There are two stages to portraying the subject – first the simple outline of the shape, and then the building up of tonal values so that the finished article looks as though it exists in its own space.

Step 2

Once you are happy with your outline drawing, make a light tone over all the areas where the shading will be, leaving untouched white paper for the highlights.

Step 3

Following this, build up more varied depths of tone to give the objects substance. Note how I have placed the flowers against a dark background to show up their brightness, and the glass vase has a much lighter background in order to make the drawing of the glass simpler. Draw all the distortions that the water and glass produce to give a convincing impression of their quality.

A Vase of Flowers in Pastel

For this pastel drawing of a vase of flowers, I worked on dark brown paper. This choice of paper adds interest as the flowers appear to glow against the dark background. For your own arrangement, you may also wish to choose flowers of different colours, lit from one side.

Step 2

Next build up all the main colours with nice definite strokes, before smudging them with a finger or a paper stub to smooth your colour areas. The vase is a deep blue, so I used a combination of cerulean on the lighter side and ultramarine on the darker side, and smudged the area where the two colours meet to help create a rounder feel to the pot. The tabletop is put in with a bit of yellow ochre on the lighter side of the table, leaving a dark brown shadow on the other side of the pot.

Step 1

First comes a simple outline of the shapes of the vase, flowers and leaves with the line of the edge of a table top in the background. Draw these outlines in the basic colours of each flower and the pot, leaves and table.

Step 3

Now you can add stronger colours to the flowers, as well as lighter blue edges to the pot. Try to get the feel of the textures of the plants as much as possible with your marks and the smoother feel of the clay pot. There is a bright highlight reflected in the surface of the pot, which you can add in white. To give the effect of light falling from the left, add a few touches of white to the flower petals, too. A little smudging of a warmer brown can be put in the background around the pot, but keep it fairly light and not too noticeable.

A Herb Planter

In this plant still life, I have shown a larger subject in the form of a planter full of herbs, such as you might have in your garden or on an allotment. The overall effect of drawing a flowerbed or planter will be less formal than a vase of flowers, though you can still focus on the contrast between the container and the luxuriant plant growth.

Step 1

Start as usual with a very loose sketch of the main shapes of the plants, getting some idea of the way that they grow and fall.

Step 2

Next comes a line drawing to put in all the leaves and stalks so that the plants are differentiated. At this stage you should make any necessary corrections – although the shapes may be changing all the time if you are working outside in the slightest breeze.

Step 3

Putting in shading will give some depth to the plants. The darkest shadows go in first, then gradually build up the different tonal areas until the result looks fairly realistic. There is no need to draw the smaller leaves exactly – just put them in with an expressive scribble. The contrast between the box and the leaves helps to make the leaves look softer and more fragile.

A Large Nature Still Life

Now comes a more challenging task – to arrange a large still life composed mainly of plants, but with a few other elements to give some balance to the composition.

I noticed some potted plants set on saucers on my windowsill that seemed to make a nice set of shapes, so I decided to use these as the main background of the picture. Next I took an arrangement of autumn leaves in a jug and placed that as the main focal point of the composition. To give a bit of variety to the foreground, I put a large squash and a couple of apples alongside the jug. Now I had a composition that mostly consisted of plant life, although in this case I didn't have any flowers on show. One of the leaves dropped off the main arrangement and lay on the table in front of the jug – a nice accidental touch. The lighting was largely from the left side, with some from behind the arrangement too.

Step 1

The stages of drawing are as before, with the first sketch defining the outside shape of the whole group, without any real detail. This enables you to get the main shape of the whole picture right before you start drawing the actual shapes of the plants.

Step 2

Then draw a careful defining line that gives you the real shapes of each leaf and stalk, and of the containers and fruit. These first two stages are where all your erasing of mistakes should take place, because it's much harder when you've got into the detail and the texture.

Step 3

Once you're happy that your drawing is on the right track, begin to fill in the tone with a single light shading over all the areas that are in shadow, including cast shadows. This gives a feeling of solidity and depth to the picture.

Step 4

Now start to deepen the tones until you have a range of tonal values that reflects how the arrangement looks. Step back from the picture occasionally to see if you have rendered the balance of tone accurately enough. Finish by making sure the darkest tones are sufficiently dark – the drawing will look weaker if they are not. Note the difference between the look of the leafy plants and the more solid surfaces of the containers and the fruit.

Master Examples

Natural subjects such as fruit and flowers have a long tradition in still-life paintings, with many 16th- and 17th-century works showing abundant arrangements of flowers or food painted with an almost botanical precision. However, since time of the Impressionists, the theme has moved on to more loosely painted pictures of great tactile beauty.

This example is after the German Renaissance artist Ludger tom Ring the Younger (1522–83). His *Vase of Flowers with White Lilies and Brown Iris Blooms* (1562) depicts a marble vase of formalistic flowers against a dark background, very decorative and one of several pictures that he produced in the same period. They were probably intended as panels for a decorative chest or wall covering.

A piece by the French painter Louise Moillon (1610–96), *Basket with Peaches and Grapes* dates from the 17th century, and shows how the single decorative theme of a basket of fruit has moved on from the piece by Ring. The handling of the surfaces of the fruit and leaves is much more convincing than that of the century before and the understanding of the shadowy parts of the composition, giving more feeling of depth to the whole picture, is notable.

In the still life of seashells on a shelf by Adriaen Coorte (*c.* 1665–1707/10), the sea is nowhere to be seen. The elegant beauty of these sea creatures' exoskeletons makes an attractive picture in its own right, apart from the pleasing connotations of the ocean.

This is a copy of a painting by Henri Fantin-Latour (1836–1904), a renowned painter from the Impressionist era. His depictions of flowers have a subtlety of texture and tactile quality that make them some of the most admired in the genre. I made my version in coloured pencils to show how such paintings can be copied with some effect in a different medium. I worked over the whole image very vigorously in order to get the depth of colour and tone as near as possible to the original. Of course it doesn't have the power of the original, but at least it gives some feeling of how well the artist saw his subject.

Moving into the late 19th century, age of change and experiment, this still life by Paul Cézanne (1839–1906) shows how artists had progressed to a point where merely representing the substance and texture of objects is no longer the main concern. Here, the left and right sides of the table are at different levels and the fruit basket is tipped up at a strange angle, giving the impression of conflicting viewpoints. In my version the rich, dense colours of oil pastels were used to capture the feel of Cézanne's original oil painting.

Pictures with a Purpose

This still life can be seen at the Medici Villa at Poggio a Caiano in Tuscany and is one of many that were painted for the powerful Medici family to depict the bounty from their own estates. Here there are about twenty paintings on the dining-room walls that catalogue every type of fruit, vegetable and animal that was produced from the estate – a sort of menu of the raw materials of what your dinner would be. My drawing is taken from about 30 varieties of lemons shown on a latticework of leaves, each group of two or three being a different variety. It almost looks like late Victorian wallpaper, except that every piece of fruit is carefully observed from nature. This is a really enormous still-life piece.

Chapter Three

TREES

Trees are such a fundamental part of the natural world, and so interesting to draw, that I have given them a chapter all to themselves. They appear in all types of settings: urban, suburban and rural, always bringing beauty and character to a place.

Drawing trees will require you to go outdoors, unless you are lucky enough to have good views of whole trees from your window. Take a hard-backed sketchbook out with you and look for trees in your local neighbourhood or park.

The main thing to learn when you come to render trees on paper is that you can never draw every single leaf – even if you did, the result would not look realistic. Concentrate instead on getting the main shape of the tree correct and the way the leaves clump together in dark masses.

In this chapter we'll look at some of the many species of trees and their characteristic shapes when in leaf. We'll also observe the textures of bark and how to draw a tree up close. The structural patterns of the trunk and branches can vary greatly, and come to the fore in the winter months when deciduous trees lose their leaves. Finally, we'll see examples of how trees have been treated in different ways by different artists, demonstrating the variety of approaches possible.

Drawing Growth and Structure

The key to drawing trees is to look at the overall shape first and sketch that in without concerning yourself over any of the detail. Don't try to draw every leaf or even every branch, because you will soon lose track of what you are doing. Stick to the most visible branches and the larger clusters of leaves.

Step 1

In your initial sketch of this pear tree, establish the outer shape of the foliage and include only the main branches. This defines the structure and will make a good basis for a drawing.

Step 2

At this stage, put in all dominant areas of shade, leaving the top clusters of leaves highlighted in the sunshine. Make the farthest branches darker in tone so they appear to recede in space. Now, build up the tones on both the foliage and the branches, using a scribbled texture of leaf shapes for the former, and marks that shade in accordance with the contours of the branches for the latter.

Look at the tree drawing below and note how the lighter parts occur at the top and the left side, but are broken up slightly by shadows, where the leaves overlie each other in large clumps. All down the right side and under the branches is in shadow, except where the side of the trunk catches the light. The tree will also cast a large shadow to the right.

Step 3

Continue to build up tone on tone, until you think that you have made a reasonable likeness of the tree in front of you.

Tree Trunks

In these examples I have focused on the trunks of large trees, noting their growth patterns and the texture of various types of bark.

Have a look at the bigger trees in your local park or, if you live out of town, in your local woods and hedgerows. Notice the strength of the root structure when it is evident above ground, like great gnarled hands clutching at the earth. Next, look closely at the bark on the main trunk and branches, then at its texture. Make sketches of what you see.

Draw a Tree in Close-up

This drawing is not of a whole tree, but of the main base area of the trunk and large branches. It is a magnificent tree, and drawing it from close up gives a sense of its size and impressive structure.

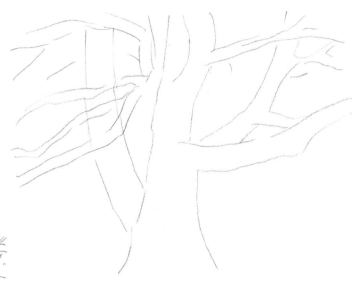

Step 1

First, draw in the main shapes of the spreading branches and the trunk, so that you have a good representation of the main shape of the tree. This will not include the ends of the branches.

Step 2

Now, as accurately as you can, draw in a simple outline of all the main shapes and this time include any leaves that come into your area of drawing. Don't try to draw every leaf – just the main masses of foliage that you can see.

Step 4

Now you can put in the darkest tones as well and you will see how this begins to give a three-dimensional feel to the whole picture. Shade only the very darkest areas at this stage.

Step 3

Next comes putting in the main tonal areas, and as you can see these are over most of the branches and trunk, which are shaded by the leaf canopy. Put them in with a uniform light tone and include the grassy ground under the shade of the tree.

Step 5

Now comes the slowest part of the drawing, where you have to blend all the necessary tones together until they begin to make more sense to the eye. Some of this will be the textural differences that you find on the trunk and branches and in the grassy area under the shadow of the tree. Continue until you feel that you have a reasonable likeness of the tree.

Trees in the Landscape

When tackling a landscape, novice artists often make the mistake of thinking they must draw every leaf. Survey a landscape with your naked eye and you will discover that you can't see foliage well enough to do this. You need to be bold and simplify. The following series of drawings is intended to help you capture the shapes of a range of common trees seen from a distance.

Getting a feel for the whole shape of the tree you want to draw is important. Often the best way to approach this is to draw in a vague outline of the main shape first. Then you need to divide this up into the various clumps of leaves and give some indication of how the main branches come off the trunk and stretch out to the final limit of the shape.

Of course, if your subject is a deciduous tree in winter the network of branches will provide the real challenge. The branches are a maze of shapes and success can only be achieved if you manage to analyse the main thrust of their growth and observe how the smaller branches and twigs hive off from the main structure. Luckily trees don't move about too much, and so are excellent 'sitters'.

These three types of deciduous tree present very different shapes and textures. Discover for yourself how different they are by finding an example of each, observing them closely and then spending time drawing the various shapes. Note the overall shapes and the branch patterns.

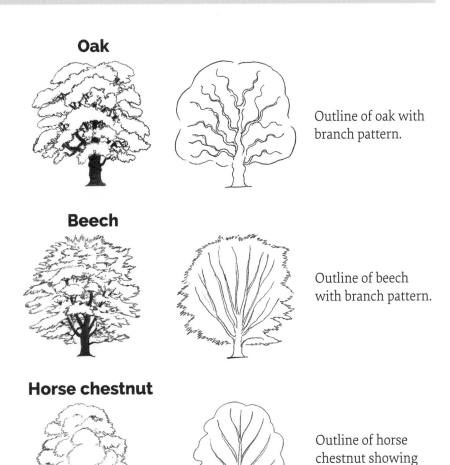

Oak

Outline of oak with branch pattern.

Beech

Outline of beech with branch pattern.

Horse chestnut

Outline of horse chestnut showing branch pattern.

ASH

By contrast with the oak and horse chestnut, the ash is much more feathery in appearance.

LOMBARDY POPLAR

The poplar is indicated by long, flowing marks in one direction, whereas with the aspen on page 82, marks have to go in all directions.

CYPRESS

The cypress holds itself tightly together in a flowing, flame-like shape; very controlled and with a sharp outline.

ELM

LIME

The elm and lime are very similar in structure. The way to tell them apart is to note the differences in the way their leaves layer and form clumps.

HOLLY

The holly tree is shaped like an explosion, its dark, spiky leaves all outward movement in an expressive organic thrust.

WALNUT

SYCAMORE

HORNBEAM

WEEPING WILLOW

ASPEN

MOUNTAIN ASH/ROWAN

OLIVE

When drawing, take note of where a darker or lighter weight of line or tone is required. Compare, for example, the weight of line needed for trees with dense dark leaves, such as the cypress and holly, with the light tone appropriate to the willow and cedar.

BIRCH

NORWAY SPRUCE

SCOTS PINE

CEDAR OF LEBANON

YEW

LARCH

PALM

Although they are of a similar family, the cedar of Lebanon and yew are easily told apart. Whereas the yew is dense and dark, the stately cedar is open-branched with an almost flat layered effect created by its canopies of soft-edged leaves.

FIG

PLANE

Branches and Patterns

Drawing branches can prove problematical for even experienced artists. The exercise below is designed to give you some practice. As before, don't worry about rendering the foliage precisely, just suggest it.

I drew this large tree in spring when its leaves were not completely out, making it an ideal subject for demonstrating the intricate tracery of branches.

When you first look at a tree like this it is not at all easy to see how to pick out each branch. One useful approach is to draw the main stems without initially worrying whether they cross in front of or behind another branch. Only when you draw a branch that crosses the first one need you make a note of whether it crosses behind or in front.

As you add more branches, the depth and space within the tree will become apparent. Ignore any leaves except as vague rounded shapes; you can add them afterwards, if you want.

When seen in silhouette every tree produces a distinctive web pattern. The point of this next exercise is to try to put in as much detail as you can, including leaves (if there are any) and twigs. To achieve this you have to draw the silhouette at a reasonable size; ie, as large as possible on an A4 sheet of paper.

One of the best varieties to choose for this exercise is a hawthorn, or May, tree. Its twisting, prickly branches and twigs make a really dense mesh, which can be very dramatic. Try drawing it in ink, which will force you to take chances on seeing the shapes accurately immediately; you are committing yourself by not being able to rub out. It won't matter too much if you are slightly inaccurate in detail as long as the main pattern is clear to you.

Winter is the best time to do this exercise, although the worst time to be drawing outdoors. You could, at a pinch, carefully copy a good photograph of such a tree in silhouette, but this would not be such a good test or teach you as much.

This silhouette is rather as you would see it against the sunlight and makes an extraordinary, intricate pattern. There is no problem with the branches being behind or in front of other branches, as there was in the example on the previous page.

Trees After Master Artists

Over the next few pages are examples showing how trees have been treated in different ways by master artists through the centuries. They demonstrate the variety of approaches possible, as well as the use of different materials to convey the feel of trees in the landscape.

This drawing after Hendrick Goltzius (1558–1617) from *Landscape Tree* (1592) demonstrates a carefully organized method of formalized textural marks in ink, which give the eye an illusion of both solidity and depth. Note how the lines trace the shapes of the tree trunks in varying ways; and how the marks that indicate the foliage repeat a feather-like texture, different from the solid parts of the trees but in the same idiom. This helps to create a harmonious effect in the drawing.

Master landscape painter Claude Lorrain (1600–82) gives a real lesson in how to draw nature in this study of a tree. Executed with much feeling but great economy, the whole drawing is done in brush and wash.

To try this you will ideally need three different sizes of brush (try Nos. 0 or 1, and 6 and 10), all of them with good points. Put in the lightest areas first (very dilute ink), then the medium tones (more ink less water), and then the very darkest (not quite solid ink).

Notice how Lorrain doesn't try to draw each leaf, but makes interesting blobs and scrawls with the tip of the brush to suggest a leafy canopy. With the heavier tones he allows the brush to cover larger areas and in less detail. He blocks in some very dark areas with the darkest tone and returns to the point of the brush to describe branches and some clumps of leaf.

Now look at this Peter de Wint (1784–1849) watercolour drawing of trees near Oxford. He has built up a grey mass of tone in rounded forms, then added darker and darker tones to give some depth to the scene. Again the best way to emulate this is to try copying him first, then draw some real trees in a similar style.

The example here, based on a work called *The Valley Farm* (1835) by the painter John Constable (1776–1837), is rather more substantial and has been produced in its copy form by first drawing the darker background trees in charcoal – smudging them to give a smoky effect – and then later drawing out the lighter shapes of the closer trees with a kneadable eraser (putty rubber). This method has produced a ghostly etched-out shape, which has then been strengthened by applying darker edges to trunk and branches, to give more apparent depth to the picture. It is a very effective technique.

This example after the British artist Ramsey Richard Reinagle (1775–1862) is in that tradition of landscape drawing where the artist draws in a refined sort of scribble, whereby Reinagle has produced a texture that resembles foliage seen from a distance. Notice that, except for the dark lines of the trunks and main branches of the trees, the rest is constructed from a closely repeated pattern of scrawling lines, rather similar to knitting. He occasionally makes it heavier but in the main he has effected a similar texture all over.

J.M.W. Turner (1775–1850) and John Constable were among the forerunners of Impressionism. In his detail from *Crossing the Brook* (1815) Turner put his trees in with a brush and the entire picture was copied one tone lighter, with all the trees and the skyline being drawn first. Then, using increasingly darker tones, the picture was built up until the trees in the foreground stood out clearly from the softer-looking background. There are about three layers of watercolour or diluted ink here.

This copy of Constable's impressionistic sketch of trees, taken from *Stoke by Nayland* (1810) was done in pencil and heavily smudged to produce a general grey tone. Then, very heavily and fairly loosely, the darker tones were built up over the main tone. If you are outside, drawing from life, do not attempt to put in any detail but just indicate the broad clumps of tonal shape.

Another example after John Constable (below), drawing in the Vale of Dedham in Suffolk. His beautifully realized clump of trees, with their intertwining branches and masses of leafy texture contrasting the hardness of the wood, is a lesson in itself.

Samuel Palmer (1805–81) portrayed the landscapes of southeast England with great skill. His drawing of oak and beech trees in the woods (see my version above) is a magnificent example of the stature that the trunk of a large tree can give to a picture, if drawn expressively. This is an exercise that you could emulate and learn a lot about drawing in the process.

These two drawings of trees after Vincent van Gogh (1853–90) take expressive mark-making to a new level.

The first drawing is of a fruit tree in Arles (1889), and here Van Gogh has drawn the trunk and main branches quite distinctly and surrounded them with a pattern of loose, scrawled marks to indicate the tree's leaves and blossom. You cannot see the foliage in any detail at all yet, somehow, the whole effect is of blossom and leaves lit up by the strong sun.

The second example is even more dramatic in its use of pattern to create the impression of foliage. Here is one of the cypresses of the Midi (St Rémy, 1889) that Van Gogh made so famous, reduced to a simple repeat pattern of swirling brush marks that seem to grow out of the ground and leap upwards into the air like flames. This reduction of shapes into a repeated texture of marks can be very effective when the artist has seen the essential quality of the object.

This example after *Burnham Beeches* by Myles Birkett Foster (1825–99) is done in coloured ink. These huge old trees with their wildly spreading branches were painted in the autumn with all the brilliance of yellow, orange, green and brown leaves, filtering the sunlight. The trees themselves appear remarkably dramatic at that time of year; the gnarled, twisted and split trunks, the interweaving branches and the brilliant foliage create a really extraordinary woodland scene.

The second scene, by another Victorian painter, W.F. Garden (1856–1921), is of willows on the River Ouse, painted in 1880. I've recreated it in pastels on beige paper. Again the drama of the twisted and split willow trunks, one of which grows downward into the stream, suggests living beings rather than trees. The wintry or early spring scene sets the bare branches like a network against the sky.

A Tree Through the Seasons

Deciduous trees go through many changes as the seasons pass. In a drawing as in reality, their appearance can tell us at once if we are looking at a winter or summer scene. From the bright green, shiny leaves of spring to the warm red, brown and gold leaves of autumn, the transformation of deciduous trees is one of the great spectacles of the natural world. Drawing a tree in each of its seasonal guises is a satisfying task, and if you choose the same tree each time, you will become familiar with its individual forms. I used coloured pencils for these examples.

We start with the tree in winter, since this allows us to see the shapes of the trunk and branches without any foliage at all. This example shows a brownish bark which has been darkened with graphite pencil to give maximum dimension to the branches and trunk. I started with the central structure, then worked out to the many fine branches and twigs that produce a pattern like a network over the space of the tree's growth. I also marked in the ground around the base and roots of the trunk to give a sense of its connection to the ground.

Next comes a version of the same tree in the spring. It has the fresh growth of the light green leaves gently scattered across the multitude of branches. There are many open spaces in the new foliage and the pushing points of the leaves outline the outer edges of the tree. The ground around the roots is also green with new grass.

Now in the midsummer, the leaves have a rich, heavier quality to them, which makes for more solid masses of dark green leaves. As you can see the bulk of the leafy cover is drawn very solidly, without many details of individual leaves. The grass under the tree is also much longer and richer in colour.

Now in the autumn, the heavy leaf bunches have drooped further and changed to a rich yellowy-brown colour. You can blend together your coloured pencils to achieve this effect. The shading on the bunches of leaves is darker and tends to break up the masses more. Some autumn leaves float gently down from the branches and the ground under the tree is covered with yellowy-brown marks resembling layers of leaf. Before too long, the tree will be back in its winter guise.

Chapter Four

EARTH, WATER AND SKY

In this section we shall focus on some of the elements that make up our natural world. When we begin to study whole landscapes, the sheer amount of material visible can be confusing and create a state of overload. It can be difficult to know where to start. A vital first step is to identify the components of a landscape. We have already looked at plants and trees in depth, and here we will learn how to draw rocks, water and sky in their various forms.

Rock formations lie underneath the vegetation and help to form the bone-structure of the landscape. Even in your garden or local park, you won't have to dig very deep before stones start to show themselves. We shall start by studying stones – their shapes and surface texture – before scaling up to larger rocky formations such as boulders, cliffs and ultimately mountains.

The element of water, if present, provides a large part of many landscapes. Still or moving, it is extremely important, on account of the brightness and reflection it gives within the general shape of the countryside. It carves out the valleys and produces the growth that makes the land look so attractive. At the edge of the land you may appreciate the spacious and mobile qualities of the sea, which again changes our view of the space in front of us.

The sky is the backdrop to everything else and is constantly changing to give a new look to the substance of the landscape. As with sea in the landscape, the sky can take up all or much of a scene or very little. Of course air itself is not visible, so we shall discover how you can convey a sense of space and atmospheric conditions through drawing various cloud formations.

Stones, Rocks and Boulders

When drawing the solid rocks that make up the surface of the earth, it can be instructive to start small and build up. Go out into your garden or local park and find some stones or pieces of rock. Pick slightly larger stones to draw first, because this will be easier than masses of small pebbles or fragments of earth.

The example shown here is a piece of pyroclastic rock, picked up on the edge of a volcanic area. Notice its overall solidity and low tonal range; it is a rather dark, non-shiny rock. The large cracks across its surface are quite dramatic, and its several facets make it a good chunky shape and not too difficult to draw.

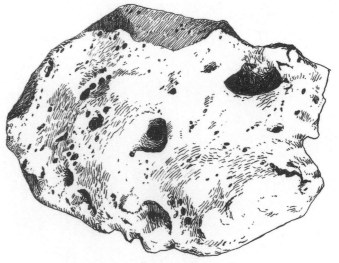

The next example is also an igneous rock, but lighter in colour and weight. This is a piece of pumice stone, often to be found in bathrooms, where it is used to smooth rough skin. Notice how the surface is covered with holes both large and small that penetrate the whole rock. It is also a light colour, so that the holes look much darker by contrast. There are fewer clearly defined facets on the surface, because being a soft rock, pumice tends to become smooth all over.

These contrasting pieces give you some idea of the variety that exists even in the humble rocks beneath your feet.

Next, turn your attention to a stony surface made up from pieces of worn rock heaped together. The main thing to notice here is how the different shapes lie in all directions, thrown together in no particular order. Notice the strong contrast between the light upper surfaces of the rocks and the deep shadows underneath.

There follows a more large-scale version of the heaps of stones, but in this case, the size of the boulders shows the varying shapes more clearly, and with more surface texture. When rendering this type of stony composition, indicate the lines of texture according to the way the various geological layers are arranged.

A Rockery in Steps

When it comes to finding larger stones and rocks to draw, a rockery in a garden or park is a good place to start. It forms a rocky landscape in miniature, and you will have the added interest of drawing the plant life growing around the rocks. My version is drawn first in pen line and then coloured.

Step 1

First, carefully denote the main shapes of the rocks and plants. At this stage, your pen line needs to be very lightly drawn without any heavy lines or marks. Make it as accurate as possible in the outer shapes of the plants and flowers.

Step 2

Next put in an initial layer of colour, using coloured pencils. Choose the main colour of each flower and rock and apply a flat colour without any real detail showing.

Step 3

Once all of your main colours are in place, you can add more detailed marks and stronger colours. Use stronger pencil marks to show the texture of the rock formations as well as extra layers of colour to differentiate between the rocks. If any element of your drawing needs extra definition, that can be achieved by using fine-liner pens over the top of your coloured pencils. I used green, orange, yellow, blue, purple and pink fine-liner pens to highlight the shapes of the leaves and flowers, giving them more intensity against the rocky background.

Rocks: Analysis

You will find these next examples useful practice for when you tackle the foreground of a mountainous or rugged landscape. They show two rocky features, drawn from a similar distance but using different media to portray the shapes and surfaces of the rocks.

In this example of a rocky outcrop, notice the very sharp black shadows cast in the cracks in the rock and the rigid angularity of the outline. I used a black marker pen to give the shadows their dramatic intensity and a combination of soft pencil and fine-liner pen for the lighter surfaces. Closer to, you would have to add more texture to the surfaces as well, but from this distance that is not so necessary.

In this example, the cracks in the surfaces and the lines of rock formation help to give an effect of the texture of the rocks and their hardness. The steps below demonstrate how to achieve this effect.

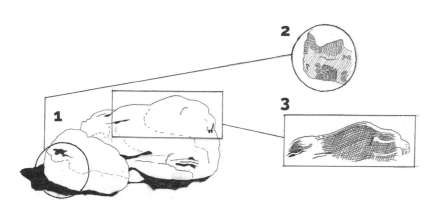

Step 1

Draw in the outline of the rocks, then put in areas of dark shadow as a solid black tone. Indicate the edges of the shaded areas by a broken or dotted line. Now carefully use cross-hatching and lines to capture the textured quality of the rock.

Step 2

These particular rocks have the striations associated with geological stratas and as these are very clearly shown you can draw them in the same way. Be careful that the lines follow the curving shape of the stone surface and when a group of them change direction, make this quite clear in your drawing. This process cannot be hurried, the variation in the shape of the rock demanding that you follow particular directions. Some of the fissures that cut through these boulders cut directly across this sequence of lines. Once again they should be put in clearly.

Step 3

Now we come to the areas of shadow which give extra dimension to our shapes. These shadows should be put in very deliberately in oblique straight lines close enough together to form a tonal whole. They should cover the whole area already delineated with the dotted lines. Where the tone is darker, put another layer of straight lines, close together, across the first set of lines in a clearly different direction.

Mountains and Cliffs

These large-scale examples show the grandeur of rocky landscapes. While you cannot apply the same detail to a cliff-face as to a single rock, you will recognize the same features of irregular surfaces and striations, on a massive scale.

If you visit a mountainous area you will see the earth in its grandest, most monumental form. This example has the added quality of being above the snow-line and showing marvellously simplified icy structures against contrasting dark rocks. When you come to tackle a landscape of this scale you will need to decide on the overall view and composition, as we shall see in Chapter 6.

Now look at a large cliff-face, with its cleavages and striations of geological layering, some of it, no doubt, partially hidden by plants, but nevertheless showing the structure very clearly.

Water and Air

These examples serve as an introduction to the next two elements in this chapter: water and air. Water shows many different qualities, from textured, choppy waves to very smooth, glassy surfaces. The element of air is principally shown through cloud formations in the sky – a crucial part of most landscape drawings.

The first example is of water so calm that you can scarcely see a ripple on the surface. The main observation is that there is very little to draw, unless there are things close by that are reflected in the surface. When the water is as calm as this, it is like drawing two pictures, the lower one a mirror-image of the one above.

Now, take a look at water that has been very slightly disturbed. Again, you get the reflections but they are broken up with so many tiny wavelets that you can see nothing clearly. The dark and light tones are there, but any sharp definition is missing.

Now, take one step further, to water that is in constant motion, thereby preventing any reflections at all. Waves breaking on to the seashore consist of a very fragmented texture, with occasional bands of thicker white surf at the edges. To draw this will be extremely demanding, not least because of the number of marks you have to make in order to convey the right effect.

Finally, on to the element of air – or at least clouds in the sky, which is principally how we observe the movement of air. The shapes are vague enough, since no cloud retains its shape for very long. However, make the clouds in your picture the softest shapes you are capable of producing. Avoid making them look too solid and hard-edged.

These two examples are fairly similar, but it should be possible to differentiate between cumulus and stratus clouds, and any variations in between.

Draw an Expanse of Water

This exercise will require your total concentration and many of the drawing skills you have acquired so far. My drawing is of a small English river, in Sussex. I haven't included much landscape around it, so the only real problem is drawing the water – but this is quite a challenge, partly because it is moving, as opposed to the flat surface of a lake on a windless day. I picked a very calm day so that the movement was reduced to a minimum.

Notice how the reflections of the bank and the building upon it are making a darker tone across the surface of the water, but everything is broken up by the ripples, which reflect the light and shade in various ways. The darker tones of the larger ripples help to define the surface, so don't hesitate to put in as many of these as you can see, but show the difference between the brighter part of the water and the darker part.

Don't be afraid to put in the very darkest tones, because one of the properties of water is to reflect the lights and darks in quite strong contrasts. It will require some judgement on your part to get the right balance of the tonal values – that is, the difference between the tones from the darkest to the lightest. Take a bit of time calculating these differences – it is never wasted.

Water: Character and Mood

The character and mood of water changes depending on how it is affected by movement and light. Over the next few pages we look at water in various forms, which present very different problems for artists and very different effects on viewers.

A waterfall is an immensely powerful form of water. Most of us don't see such grand works of nature as this magnificent example. Of course, you would need to study one as large as this from a distance to make some sense of it. This drawing is successful largely because the watery area is not overworked, but has been left almost blank within the enclosing rocks, trees and other vegetation. The dark tones of the vegetation throw forward the negative shapes of the water, making them look foaming and fast-moving.

Unless you were looking at a photograph, it would be almost impossible to draw with any detail the effect of an enormous wave breaking towards you as you stood on a shore.

This is water as most of us who live in an urban environment see it; still and reflective. Although the surface of a stretch of water may look smooth, usually there is a breeze or currents causing small shallow ripples. Seen from an oblique angle these minute ripples give a slightly broken effect along the edges of any objects reflected in the water. When you draw such a scene you need to gently blur or break the edges of each large reflected tone to simulate the rippling effect of the water.

In this very detailed drawing of a stretch of water rippling gently, there appear to be three different tones for the smooth elliptical shapes breaking the surface. This is not an easy exercise but it will teach you something about what you actually see when looking at the surface of water.

In this view of a choppy inky sea, with breaking crests of foam, the skyline is dark and there is no bright reflection from the sky. The shapes of the foaming crests of the wind-blown waves are very important. They must also be placed carefully so that you get an effect of distance, with large shapes in the foreground graduated to smaller and smaller layers as you work your way up the page towards the horizon.

Observe how foam breaks; take photographs and then invent your own shapes, once you've seen the typical shapes that are made. No two crests of foam are alike, so you can't really go wrong. But, if you are depicting a stormy sea, it is important to make the water between the crests dark, otherwise the effect might be of a bright, albeit breezy, day.

This whole drawing is made up of the sky and its reflection in the river below. The lone boat in the lower foreground helps to give a sense of scale. Although the trees are obviously quite tall in this view, everything is subordinated to the space of the sky, defined by the clouds, and the reflected space in the water. The boat and a few ripples are there to tell the viewer that it is water and not just air. The effect of this vast space and mirror is to generate awe in the viewer.

A Small Landscape with Water

This short project is intended to get you thinking about how you might tackle a small landscape with water. I took a trip to a wetlands nature reserve beside the River Thames in south-west London. The environment is especially dedicated to the flora and fauna of watery and marshy places, so although it isn't quite wilderness, it has a natural feel.

Step 1

After exploring various places around the reserve, I decided to opt for this view across an expanse of stream with many silver birches and other marsh-loving trees scattered along the banks. At first I sketched in the main areas of the composition very simply so that I knew how much I was going to take on.

Step 2

Then I worked up the details of the trees and the water in a linear fashion so that I had the whole scene drawn up clearly and could make any alterations as I felt necessary. I used loose, zig-zagging marks to indicate the reflections of the trees and vegetation on the surface of the water.

Step 3

To finish the drawing I carefully put in the tonal values so that the water and trees began to show more depth and spatial qualities. This is quite a simple scene in terms of composition, but the flimsy quality of the winter trees where I could see through their branches was quite a challenge – a very light touch was needed. To achieve the smooth tonal quality of the water I used a very soft pencil (7B) and smudged the marks with my finger.

Water: Master Examples

In a landscape, the presence of water gives a new liveliness to the scene, both in its reflection of the sky and the vegetation and its mobile, rippling surface, which is rarely still. To complete our investigation of water, study this selection of watery scenes after master artists.

These examples show trees reflected in water. On the right is the snowy scene *Winter Evening by a River* by Gustav Fjaestad (1868–1948), in which the water reflects the trunks of the adjacent trees in dark and light swirls. Broken reflections in running water are a difficult but very interesting effect to attempt to draw and you can try it in any season.

This simplified version of *The Seine at Giverny* by Claude Monet (1840–1926) shows a rather more summery scene of trees reflected in water, which he produced in a range of blues, greens and whites. Our version gives a dramatic effect with the almost monochrome range of strong blues and whites, executed in pastels, which can look very similar to oil paints. The bright gap of white sky seen through the heavily shaded trees is reflected rather less sharply in the water. The greens and blues of the trees are also reflected there, less defined in a more generalized colour splash. It is a very rich and dramatic picture, although tranquil at the same time.

Now for a scene with running water taken from Joseph Wright of Derby's (1734–97) version of Rydal Lower Falls. Although the scene has hardly changed to this day, our re-creation of it in coloured pencil probably doesn't have quite the power of his, which is partly due to the medium. It is a good medium for gradation and variety in colour, but not so punchy in effect as other media.

Artist's Tip

The thing to remember about water is the intense contrast between the lit parts and the darker, shadowed areas. This contrast is part of water's charm and always lends a sparkle to a landscape. You will need to study moving water quite carefully, and the use of a camera is a great asset here. But don't just slavishly copy the camera version – it always helps if you have spent some time carefully studying moving water and getting a feel for the way it looks.

These examples show views of water seen from very different viewpoints. In this version of Monet's *Railway Bridge at Argenteuil* (1874), the viewpoint is down near the level of the river, with the bridge and the nearby trees and bushes looming above. The puffing, rolling steam from the railway engine pours off the bridge, the broad piers of which appear almost too big for the minimal construction it supports. The reflections also help to emphasize the height of the bridge over the rest of the scene.

The higher your viewpoint, the larger and grander the landscape you can encompass. This picture, after the painting of the Niagara Falls by Heinrich Fuseli (1741–1825), is possibly one of the largest and grandest landscapes you could ever draw. I have used a mixture of watercolour and coloured inks to recreate it. First, I layered some flat areas of watercolour and then drew in a few details in coloured inks to define the scene more clearly. The position of the artist was high enough to observe the whole sweep of Niagara, plus the distant landscape with the river winding its way towards the Falls from the Great Lakes. In the original, Fuseli had the figure of a Native American standing in the foreground to give some idea of scale, but the tall pine trees on the lower bank give a decent sense of scale as well.

The Sky: Contrasts

Air is invisible, of course, so cannot really be drawn, but it can be inferred by looking at and drawing clouds and skyscapes. Whether fluffy, ragged, streaky or layered, clouds give a shape to the movements of the elements in the sky and are the only visible evidence of air as a subject to draw.

Here we see dark, stormy clouds with little bits of light breaking through in areas around the dark grey. The difficulty is with the subtle graduations of tone between the very heavy dark clouds and the parts where the cloud cover is thinner or partly broken and allows a gleam of light into the scene. Look carefully at the edges of the clouds, how sometimes they are very rounded and fluffy and sometimes torn and ragged in shape. If you get the perspective correct, they should be shown as layers across the sky, flatter and thinner further off and as fuller more rolling masses closer to. You can create a very interesting effect of depth and space across the lower surfaces of the cloudscape with bumps and layers of cloud that reduce in depth as they approach the horizon.

When the clouds allow more sun to shine through, they look much less heavy and threatening and often assume quite friendly-looking shapes. Essentially, though, it is the same vapour as in the stormy sky but with more light, enabling us to see its ephemeral nature.

Showing beams of sunlight striking through clouds can have a remarkable effect in a picture, and can give a feeling of life and beauty to even a quite banal landscape.

A lot has been achieved here with very simple means. The clouds are not complicated and it is the sun's rays (marked in with an eraser) and the aircraft that do much of the work, giving the illusion of height and also limitless space above our view. The broken light, the light and dark clouds and sunlight glinting against the wings and fuselage of the aircraft give the drawing atmosphere.

The Sky: Using Space

The spaces between clouds as well as the shapes of clouds themselves can alter the overall sense we get of the subject matter in a drawing. The element of air gives us so many possibilities, we can find many different ways of suggesting space and open views. Compare these examples.

This open flat landscape with pleasant soft-looking clouds gives some indication of how space in a landscape can be implied. The fluffy cumulus clouds floating gently across the sky gather together before receding into the vast horizon of the open prairie. The sharp perspective of the long, straight road and the car in the middle distance tell us how to read the space. This is the great outdoors.

Another vision of air and space is illustrated here: a sky of ragged grey and white clouds, and the sun catching distant buildings on the horizon of the flat, suburban heathland below. Note particularly the low horizon, clouds with dark, heavy bottoms and lighter areas higher in the sky.

Despite the presence of dark, dramatic clouds in this scene at sunset the atmosphere is not overtly gloomy or brooding. The bright sun, half-hidden by the long flat cloud, radiates its light across the edges of the clouds, which tell us that they are lying between us and the sun. The deep space between the dark layers of cloud gives a slightly melancholic edge to the peacefulness.

A Dramatic Sky: Practice

Here is a large dramatic sky, after Constable, depicting a rainstorm over a coastal area, with ships in the distance. The sweeping linear marks denoting the rainfall give the scene its energy. The effect of stormy clouds and torrential rain sweeping across the sea is fairly easily achieved, as long as you don't mind experimenting a bit. Your first attempt might not be successful, but with a little persistence you will soon start to produce interesting effects, even if they are not exactly accurate. This type of drawing is great fun. Keep going until you get the effect you want.

Step 1

For the first stage, use a fine pen with a bit of flexibility in the nib and black ink. Scribble in vertical and wind-blown lines to suggest heavy rainfall. The sea can be marked in using both fine horizontal strokes and more jagged, fairly strong wave-like marks. To complete the effect, dip a hogs-hair brush into dark watercolour paint and splatter this across areas of the picture. This produces a more uneven texture to suggest agitated sea and rain.

Step 2

Then, using one large and one small brush (ideally hog's hair brushes, which have a stiff texture), put in pale washes of watercolour across the sweep of the rain and horizontally across the sea. Repeat this with a darker tone until you get the effect you require in the sky and sea. Allow the brush to dry out periodically and then apply almost dry brush marks to accentuate the effect of unevenness or patchiness.

Bringing Elements Together

Over the next few pages we'll see how the elements of earth, water and air can be combined in very different landscapes, from dramatic to serene.

This drawing, after *View from Table Rock* by W.H. Bartlett (1809–54), shows a part of the Niagara Falls seen from below Table Rock. It is a splendid evocation of the great outdoors. The drama of the dark rock face hanging over, and framing, the right half of the picture makes for extreme contrast, both in darkness and light, and between grim solidity and wild movement. To underline the massive size of this natural phenomenon, the artist has placed a tiny figure on the rock in the foreground, to give a sense of scale.

This landscape drawn in mixed media shows a very different type of view, with an evenly balanced, serene-looking composition and a slightly stylized depiction of the water and hills. This is a relatively easy landscape to reproduce, for which you can use pencil or charcoal and pen and ink. Use the pencil or charcoal softly to smudge in the clouds (you can even smudge your marks with a paper napkin to give a very soft effect) and then draw with the pen the outlines of the mountains and the strongest reflections of them. Fill in some of the darker areas with ink but don't overdo it. Then with the pencil or charcoal, tone in the large dark areas and smudge it again to get softer effects. You will have to make stronger pencil marks close to the pen lines or else they will not blend in with the main shape. Finally, the lighter part of the reflecting water can again be smudged in with pencil or charcoal.

This example of a scene in Richmond Park close to London is made in watercolour, showing the sun just disappearing behind some large trees. I've kept the colour light on the ground areas and darker and richer on the trees, with the focus on the bright sunset in the centre of the picture. Using watercolour to show the sunset will require some practice, as you need to ensure there is no sharp break between the area of pinkish glow around the sun's orb and the light blue in the rest of the sky. Use plenty of water and larger brushes, working as quickly as you can so that the colour areas mix smoothly. By contrast, you can leave the watercolour to dry before you draw in the deep orange of the sun itself. For the ground cover in the bottom half of the picture, mix some yellow into your browns and greens to show the warmth of the sun's rays. See page 206 for more tips on creating a watercolour landscape.

The sea takes up two-thirds of this picture, which shows a wide bay with rocky cliffs enclosing a flat beach on Lanzarote. The sweep of the sea from the horizon to the surf on the beach creates a very pleasant and restful depth to the drawing. The close-up of rocky boulders adds a touch of connection to the onlooker, as does the viewpoint, which suggests we are viewing the scene from high up on the cliff.

A detailed pencil landscape like this requires you to vary your mark-making to portray the different elements of water, sky, sand and rocks. Light hatched lines on the beach show the pull of the sea on the sand, and clear outlines and deep shadows denote the jagged rocks in the foreground (rocks like this should be tackled in the same way as the boulders on page 105).

This drawing of Lake Tahoe in California is done in coloured pencils and has a soft, misty look. The sky and background shoreline are pale and bluish, contrasting with the darker spit of shoreline jutting into the lake, coloured in deep, dark green. The nearer part of the lake is light ultramarine blue fading to a pale yellow on the beach in the right-hand corner. The island in the middle looks dark and almost purple. In the foreground, I used my pencil to accentuate the jagged structures of the rocks and wall, in stark contrast to the smooth surface of the lake.

Chapter Five

ANIMALS

Animals are great fun to draw and present very different challenges to many of the other subjects covered in this book. One major difference is that, unlike plants and trees, many animals won't stay still long enough for you to make more than a quick sketch. This means that, when drawing from life, you have to start drawing quickly and go for only the most obvious shapes first, even in the case of a sleeping animal, as most tend to move quickly once awake. This is an area of drawing where photography is particularly useful, especially for supplementing swift sketches done at the same time. Taking photographs of animals in similar poses to the ones you have tried to capture will give you more information to do a finished drawing.

We shall start by looking at small animals with a relatively simple structure, such as insects, birds, small mammals and fish. We shall explore how you can render texture in your drawings, whether your subject has soft fur or glistening scales. Moving on to slightly larger animals, many of us have cats and dogs at home and they are undoubtedly a very good source of animal study, as are farm animals such as cows, sheep and horses. Sooner or later you will probably want to try your hand at a really large creature such as an elephant or a lion, when a trip to a zoo will be very instructive.

Once familiar with the shapes of an animal, the next task is to convey some semblance of movement. You can experiment right from the start with techniques for getting the animals to appear more convincing; a drawing doesn't have to be precise in order to create the feeling of an animal in action. An expressionist technique is more likely to conjure up the essence of an animal than a careful, detailed drawing. But whatever you draw from the immense range of animal life, have fun experimenting with various ideas and effects.

Small Forms

Insects are a good place to start when drawing animals. Most insects have a very simple structure, with their skeleton on the outside, so you can draw them almost diagrammatically. Move on to small animals and birds, which also have quite simple shapes. Observing live animals is the best way to understand how their bodies are constructed and how you can make your drawings come to life. If you live near a museum with a natural history section, that would also be a good place to augment your knowledge of animal form.

Starting with the world of insects, you may have more or less luck depending on the area that you live in. Here I show a tiger beetle, which is a fairly straightforward insect shape, but larger than many other insects and therefore easier to draw. The main thing in this case is to get the basic shape right and there won't be much need for subtle details.

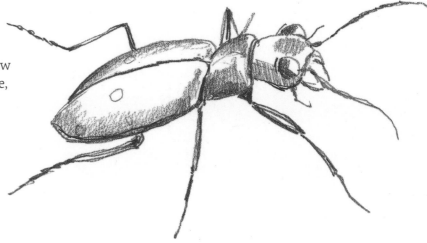

Next, we have a frog which is small, but more solid and compact, and the texture or colour of the animal will help to give a more convincing feel to your drawing. Achieving a good outline is most important in order to convey the character of the creature through your drawing.

Next, a bird with distinctive markings. This lapwing also has a nice crest, which lends it further character.

A field mouse is basically a little furry ball with ears and a long tail. I see these sometimes in our suburban garden, when our young cat catches one to play with, and I have to rescue it and put it back in the flower beds.

These two birds are quite common around my home area. The crow can be drawn almost as a silhouette, with just a few lighter patches showing highlights on its glossy feathers.

The sparrow is not so dark as the crow, with clear markings. The outline shape and the main colour change does it all.

Shape and Colour

Animals and colour are interesting, because many animals have such extremely strong colour combinations that you can really start to enjoy yourself in representing them accurately. Of course in northern climates you get a lot of rather subdued colour, but in more tropical zones, colour is often quite extravagant. So look around for the most interesting animals that you can find and learn to put in your colour with confidence and enjoyment.

If you have access to a natural history display, find a range of mounted moths and butterflies to draw at your leisure. The example shown here is a Monarch butterfly, which I have produced by first laying down an area of yellow-orange watercolour and then drawing over the top of it in black ink. Because the shape presents itself with a flat surface, there is no problem of representing depth, which gives you an easier start.

The next example is from the bird kingdom, showing the characteristic shape of the mallard drake. It can be kept as a silhouette without any need to show depth. The patches of colour are well defined and the whole drawing has a very clear pattern and decorative feel to it. You simply draw in each area of colour with the brush and fit them together like a neatly slotting puzzle.

Now we look at two more bird drawings – done in coloured pencil – of a goldfinch and a rainbow parakeet. Once again, thanks to their colour patterning, you do not need to pay much attention to the solidity of the creatures. Keep the areas of colour fairly flat and the combination of brilliant colour and design will be sufficient to give a very attractive impression of the types of bird that you have drawn.

Artist's Tip

When painting or drawing in colour where the colour is flat and unmodulated, it is often best to outline the shape first and then fill in the colour. Draw the outline in the same medium that will be used for the main colour, or outline in very light pencil, which you can afterwards rub out. You can also draw the outline in pencil or ink on a separate piece of paper, and then put it with another on a light box or on a window and trace the shape through in the main colour.

Draw a Seagull in Steps

Unlike most birds, seagulls sometimes stand still for long enough to make good subjects. Even if one bird moves away, another similar one will probably be close by.

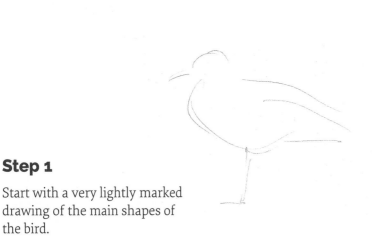

Step 1

Start with a very lightly marked drawing of the main shapes of the bird.

Step 3

Next, put in the main areas of shade with an evenly light tone. Leave a dot of unshaded paper to make a highlight in the bird's eye.

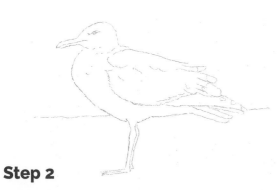

Step 2

Then make a more accurate outline so that you have got all the main parts indicated in the drawing.

Step 4

Then turn to the very darkest tones, which are mainly some of the edges, the eye and the very dark tail feathers.

Step 5

Finally, work carefully over the whole shape, putting in all the variations of tone as accurately as you can.

Portraying Texture

The following examples focus on the particular textures of the animals chosen. Selecting a suitable medium can help to convey the qualities of an animal's fur, shell, scales or skin.

The rabbit has been drawn in pastel, and the soft smudgy shapes go very well with the furry pelt of the animal. Pastel lends a textural quality, which emphasizes the way that this animal is perceived by touch as well as by sight.

The crab is smoother and harder than the rabbit, and connected
with water, so watercolour here seems to be a good idea. Don't
forget to let the first colour dry if you want sharp edges to any
subsequent colour.

Draw a Catfish in Steps

In this example, your aim is to capture the glistening surface of the catfish scales, as well as its distinctive mottled markings. The key is to leave areas of highlight and to smudge and blend your pencil marks.

Step 1

First make a loose outline of the fish, which has an easy enough shape to follow.

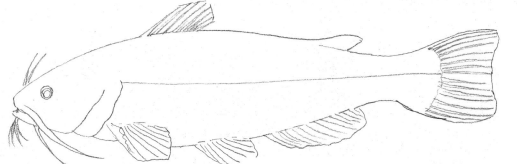

Step 2

Next make a more careful, precise outline that gives you all the detail you need.

Step 3

Put light tone all over the fish except for the highlights, which are essential to convey the shiny skin.

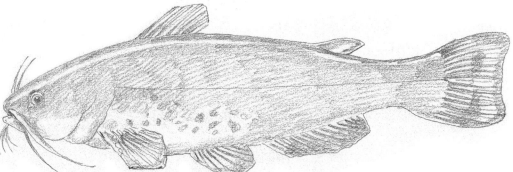

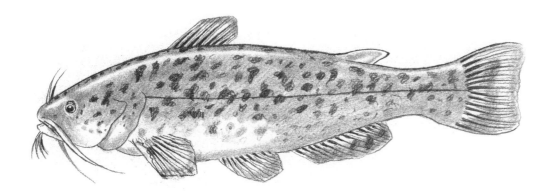

Step 4

Add the very darkest areas next, to define the fish further. These are mainly the markings on the skin and the striations on the fins and tail.

Step 5

Work the mid-tones all over the fish to give more subtlety to its appearance. To increase the shiny effect of the skin, smudge and blend the softer areas of shade.

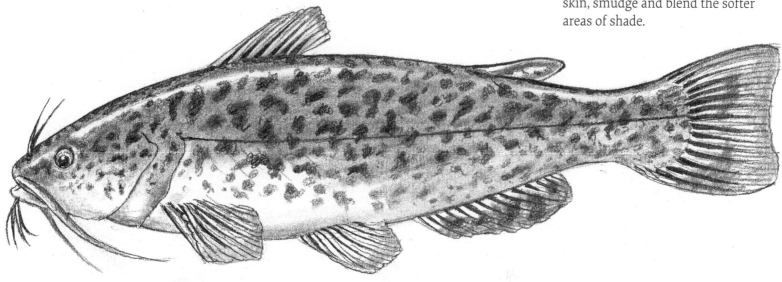

Cats

Domestic cats are very useful models as they are very somnolent – most sleep for about 16 hours a day. Consequently, you should have plenty of time for fairly detailed studies and because of their furry coat and relaxed, graceful forms they tend to present easy, fluid shapes to draw.

Draw the main shape of the body in a very simple way, as you can see in these examples, and add the heads and legs to that.

Next, show the texture of the fur with multiple strokes of the pencil. Indicating the coat markings will make the drawing look much more like a portrait of that particular animal. The eyes and nose are important, and as they are very close to each other you shouldn't find it too difficult to see the right proportions.

When you feel confident enough, have a try at more active animals and see how far you can take the drawing. Go for the main outline first and then as much as you can include in the time you've got.

Once you have made a few sketches, you will feel confident in trying something more complex. Here is where a decent photograph of a cat in action could go a long way towards making your next attempt quite realistic. Using the photograph as reference, and ideally with the animal still around where you can see him, you can start on an authentic representation of a cat on the prowl. Mine is done in coloured inks, because the texture of the fur lends itself to this multi-stroke technique. So using grey, brown, green, yellow and black, you too can build up a convincing effect.

For this posed picture of a beautiful long-haired cat, start by drawing in the main area of its body, head and tail, just to indicate the size and shape. Once you are happy with the main shapes, begin to add the fluffy fur over the main shape and the legs, and the features of the face. Add the darkest tones of the striped fur and around the eyes last.

Dogs

Dogs spend less time asleep than cats but, while awake, tend to be much more co-operative. They vary much more in appearance, so you will need to check the proportions with each new breed to make it recognizable. As before, draw the main shape simply at first and add detail in the time you have available.

Drawing a dog in its basket is certainly easier while it sleeps, although dogs do often move while asleep. So draw the dog in first and the shape of the basket after, as the dog may wake up and move off. If working in coloured pencil, delineate the main areas of colour on the dog's coat first, then fill them in using strokes of colour in the same direction as the fur.

Farm Animals

Have a go at drawing farm animals if you are in the countryside, or even in town if there is a city farm near by.

Luckily sheep and cows don't move too fast, and they keep adopting the same poses. Note the different characteristics belonging to the breed rather than just reproducing your idea of what a cow or sheep should look like. Practice makes perfect, so keep your sketchbook with you wherever possible and even if you have only two or three minutes to do a thumbnail sketch it is still excellent drawing practice.

Horses

Along with large farm animals like cows, horses are probably one of the easiest large animals to find for drawing from life. You may have to draw from photographs for this exercise, but if you are near stables, do take the opportunity to draw from life as much as you can.

Drawing horses from life is not too difficult but they do gently move around, and so most of your drawing will resemble the first two sketches shown on the right. However after drawing several sketches like these you may be able to get some more detail as the horse takes up similar positions.

Horses are an excellent subject because you can see many of the muscles through the smooth coat. Start as before, getting the main shapes down first; that is often the most you can do, unless you have the chance to draw a tethered horse, when you can mark in the large, well-developed muscles that most horses display.

As you add detail to your drawing, don't be afraid to mark the muscles in strongly and quickly – you can treat them with a greater degree of subtlety when you are more practised.

This drawing is my own version of a famous painting of a great horse, *Whistlejacket* by George Stubbs (1724–1806). I've used pastel here and kept it fairly loose in style so that the marvellously lively horse doesn't become too stilted. The shine on the animal's coat and the ripple of the light-coloured tail and mane give some idea of the beautiful original, which of course is very large and kept in the National Gallery in London.

Draw a Horse in Steps

A horse's prime motivation is to graze, so you should have no difficulty in sustained studies of them doing that – it's an alert pose with the head up that you have to be fast to capture. Photographing them at the same time gives you extra information that you can add to your drawings later.

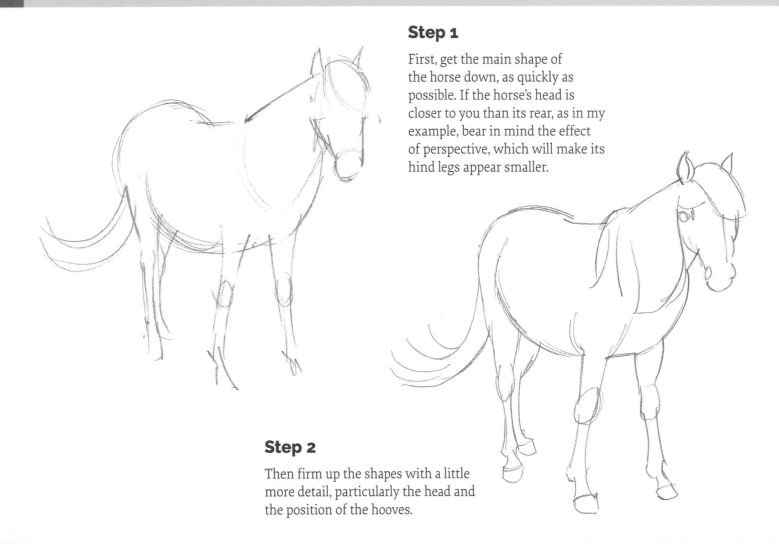

Step 1

First, get the main shape of the horse down, as quickly as possible. If the horse's head is closer to you than its rear, as in my example, bear in mind the effect of perspective, which will make its hind legs appear smaller.

Step 2

Then firm up the shapes with a little more detail, particularly the head and the position of the hooves.

Step 3

Finally, add details of tone and texture to help give a more solid look. Some areas, like between the legs near the chest and on the ears and nose, can be put in more intensely to contrast with the white areas on the horse's flank.

Animals in Motion

Observing an animal and understanding how it moves is a good first step to portraying movement, as well as studying photographs and the work of other artists. When you come to draw, choose a medium to fit the subject and keep your style loose to convey the feeling of movement.

Here is a frog drawn poised to hop, his shape looking somewhat jerky and awkward in comparison with the graceful lines of the horse on page 157. However, you can approach a subject like this in exactly the same way as you would the horse, keeping the style simple and loosely drawn, in order to give some semblance of movement to the finished product.

Next I show a lizard in mid-scamper. It has a straightforward shape and, as long as the texture of the skin looks scaly enough, there are no great drawing problems here either. The colour can be kept to a minimum, with just enough to hint at the green, sinuous body.

The following drawings
continue with the notion
of movement and how to
reproduce it, but this time I
have used coloured pencils in an
effort to gain the right effect.

The arctic tern is contrasted
against the pure blue sky and
this use of a plain background
colour certainly helps to set
off the movement of the bird
in flight. The tern itself is put
in very sketchily with no clear
details, just as you would see it if
it were to fly past you suddenly.

In the next picture, I have a leopard
running forward to pounce on its
prey. The drawing is similar in style
to the bird, in that the lines defining
the animal are loosely drawn to give
some idea of the powerful muscular
activity of the beast. I decided not
to represent the leopard's spots very
accurately but merely suggested the
arrangement of their pattern as this
all helps to give an impression of the
animal moving at speed.

The next picture is of an American bald eagle, which is the emblem of the USA. I have drawn this one with a brush, in watercolour, and tried to keep it straightforward in style, with all the emphasis on the outspread wings and the arrow-like body. Only two colours were used but you could play around with blacks and browns and other tints, as long as you don't lose the active effect of the flying bird.

Another animal is on the move in the next picture – this time it is a fox loping across a meadow with the moon rising in the background. I have splashed in the foxy red of his coat without attempting too distinct a shape, putting dark patches of colour on the feet, nose and ears, and leaving quite a bit of white showing around the muzzle and on the tip of the tail. You will have to be a little more careful when it comes to putting in the green pasture and the sky, making sure you stay clear of the fox's outline, so there is no danger of the colours running.

In this example, we have a dolphin leaping out of the water in a shining arc. The movement here is suggested by the very curve of the creature. The effect of the waves below it and the wet shine on the body help to convince the viewer that the scene is drawn from live observation.

More Unusual Animals

Unless you go to a safari park, animals such as lions and elephants usually have limited opportunity to move about much and you may not have a wide choice of viewpoint. However, you should find a range of poses to draw. As you will be viewing these animals from a distance, detail is less important than with domestic animals, but inform your drawings with photographic reference as well to help your accuracy.

The elephant is a large enough animal to be drawn with smooth, fluid lines, adding areas of tone where the deepest shadows are, such as inside the huge ears and beneath the trunk.

Once again, draw the main outline shape, before the animal moves too much. Even if you are working from photographs, use the same method.

Next, firm up the structure of the animal, putting in more details of the head and the large muscles. Note how the well-defined, high cheekbone adds to the lion's majestic appearance.

Herds of Animals

Drawing animals in larger numbers may strike you as harder at first, but in fact it can be easier. One of the most significant things about herds and flocks is that all their members share the same habits, so when one moves out of a pose that you are drawing another will conveniently adopt a very similar position, giving you a chance to complete your work.

Here I have shown herds of deer and sheep and, to change the task slightly, a flock of seagulls. The latter group is harder in one way because of course they are in constant movement. However, their shapes are relatively simple and they all swirl around in much the same way, so that after a while you begin to see how you can draw them more easily.

Sheep are fairly slow in their movements, and among the most docile of your models. Deer, on the other hand, are rather nervous of people getting close to them, but because you will have to draw them from some way off you will more easily be able to reduce their shapes to the simplest formula.

An Animal Drawing After Rousseau

In composing this picture I have taken my inspiration from 'Le Douanier' Rousseau (1844–1910) because his work is so imaginative. The scene can be set by drawing enlargements of plants from your own garden or house plants, or by working from photographic reference. The animal needs to be an exotic type, like a tiger, to fit in with Rousseau's fantastical scenes.

Step 1

You will need to study plants close up, although you do not need to have access to real jungle plants because quite ordinary ones will do, as long as you make them look much bigger than they actually are. Vary the shapes of leaves a little and make them look more luxuriant. Having got enough in the way of leaves, find some type of flower to be your jungle blossoms. Choose something florid and pink or red.

Step 2

Then make some drawings of a tiger or some other exotic animal in a prowling pose. It is probably easiest to work from photographs.

Step 3

Having got your plants and wild animal, the only thing left to do is to design your picture, by sketching the main outlines of the scheme. You can produce the details as you go along – it's more fun and probably produces better results in this type of picture. Don't hold back on the colour.

Step 4

Using a toned paper to draw on, and pastels for their rich colour values, you can construct a jungle landscape where plant shapes jostle and overlap each other.

Reserve a little space for the sky and show this in a deep azure colour with the sun or moon glowing brightly. Make the most of the decorative values of the plant shapes and the animal's markings – don't try to be too realistic. The whole charm of this type of picture is in its decorative, dream-like richness.

Artist's Tip

Drawing with pastels, you have a greater colour range at your disposal than for anything else, except paint. You will find it most advantageous to work on toned or coloured paper, and there are many kinds available, from cheap sugar paper to more expensive stock, such as Canson or Ingres papers. Any art shop stocks a variety of sheets and pads and, if you enjoy working with pastels, it is worth trying out several different surfaces until you find the one that suits you best. One pastel artist I know of draws straight onto thick board and I have many times worked on ordinary brown or grey cardboard.

Chapter Six

LANDSCAPE BASICS

I've made landscape the last topic to explore in detail because it's probably the most ambitious, bringing together many of the elements we've looked at so far in this book.

Never forget that the world is three-dimensional and that your eyes see it as such. When we commit a view of the world on to a flat surface such as paper, we have to employ techniques to give the illusion of depth, distance and spaciousness. We shall start this section by looking at how perspective works and how you can use it in your landscapes.

When tackling a landscape the artist's first task is to select a view, to decide on how much of that view to show, and from which angle. When you survey a landscape full of trees, bushes and grass, take time to look at each area of vegetation carefully and note the immense variety of textures and colour that exist in just one view. Before choosing your landscape, decide how much detail you want to include and how much of a feeling of space you want to give it. Adjust your viewpoint to achieve this, by lowering it to get closer, or lifting it to create a greater sense of distance. In this chapter you will find examples of how to explore an area and choose your viewpoint, as well as practical tips such as using a landscape frame or taking photographs to use at home.

Enjoy the qualities of the natural world when you are drawing in the countryside or in a local garden or park. Don't worry if the piece doesn't always go right. The fun is in finding out how to do it in practice and, eventually, you reach the stage when you just draw the whole thing by eye and you can forget about the science.

Perspective

Before starting any larger landscape scene, it is useful to have an understanding of the laws of perspective. This is the technique of making a two-dimensional drawing – with length and breadth – appear to have a third dimension – that of depth.

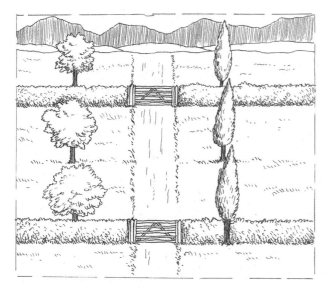 

In very simple terms, you can see the difference between the two pictures shown above, one drawn without much attention to perspective, and the other based on the system of single point perspective, which tricks the eye into thinking that it is seeing depth and space.

Note how the trees and gateways are all the same size in the first picture, whether they are close to the viewer or far away. Also, look at how the road stays the same width even as far as the horizon; nor is there much difference between the texture of the nearest trees and hedges and those further off. The result is the effect of a rather flat landscape.

The second version shows what happens when you devise a method of interpreting the same landscape seen in terms of space. The nearest objects are both larger and more textured than those further away, and already this gives a sense of depth to the picture. The road appears to narrow as it recedes into the distance, eventually disappearing to a single point far off on the horizon. Although this is a fairly simple drawing the effect is immediate.

So, how do you achieve it?

The cone of vision

When we look at any view, there is a field of vision surrounding us that can be divided into the area where we see things clearly and – at the periphery – another area where we can hardly define anything at all. The overall effect is to create a 'cone' of vision, within which we can see objects clearly, and outside which we are aware of nothing except light and darkness.

In the diagram, a figure is standing at a point in space called the 'station point'. From this point, the figure looks straight ahead at the centre line of vision. The horizon is naturally at eye level, and where the line of vision cuts across the horizon is the centre point of an area that includes everything one can see of the space in front. The circle of vision is that part of the cone of vision that meets with what is known as the 'picture plane'. And this is the area upon which all your images are to be drawn. It is usually perpendicular to the ground plane of the surface on which you stand. The picture plane covers an area containing all that could go into your picture. Of course, you might choose to crop down your picture area, but it is possible to draw anything within the focus of this space.

When you come to compose a picture based on this theory of vision, in a way you reverse the process and construct a series of shapes based on the centre point, which becomes the 'vanishing point'. Overleaf I explain how to create this one-point perspective.

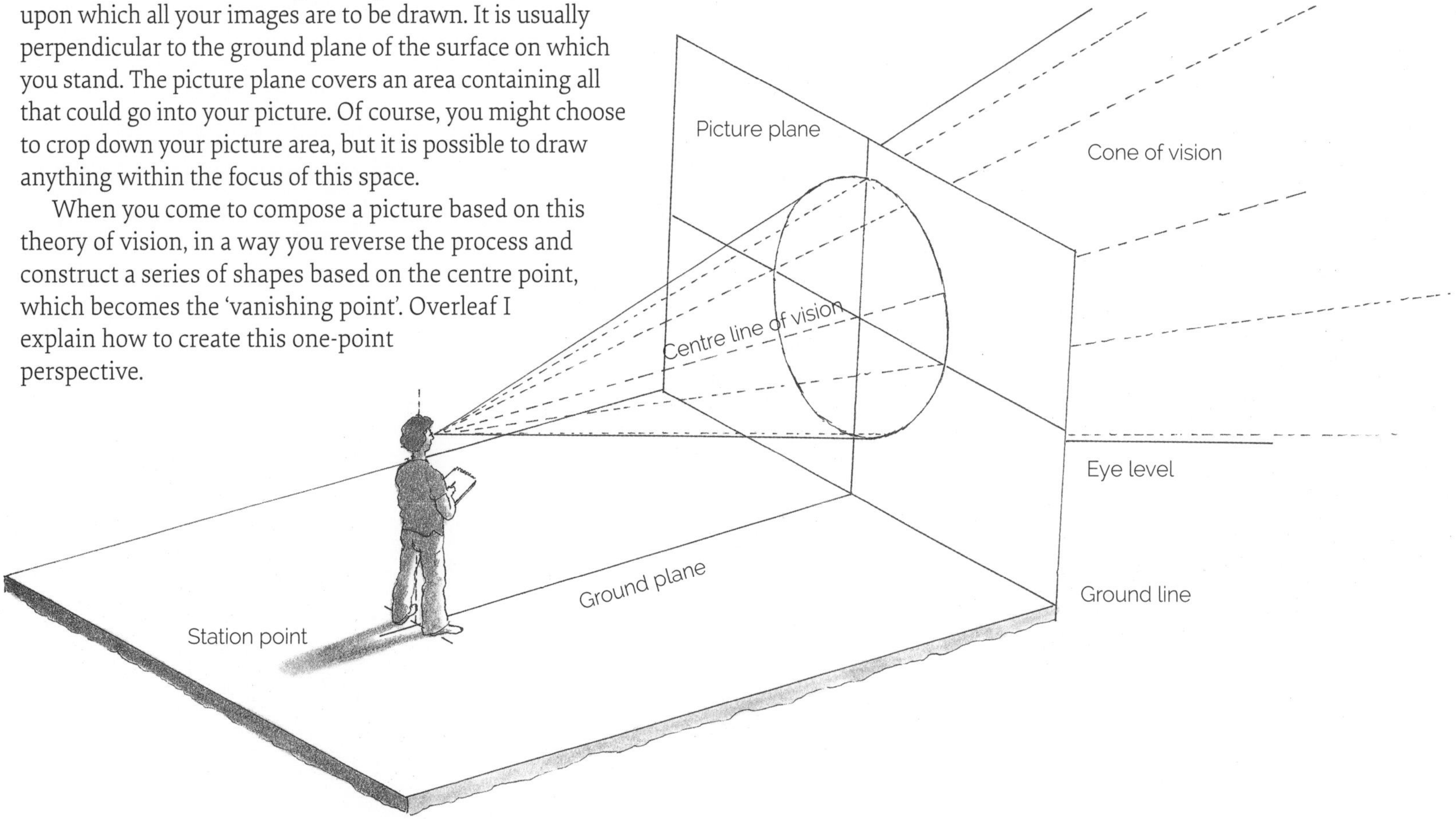

Picture plane

Cone of vision

Centre line of vision

Eye level

Ground plane

Ground line

Station point

One-point Perspective

The most simple and obvious type of perspective is one-point perspective, where all the lines of the landscape will appear to diminish to a single point (the vanishing point) right in front of your view on the far horizon. You only get this type of perspective when the objects between you and the horizon are fairly uniformly distributed and any buildings are not too obvious.

Draw a horizon line from one side of the paper to the other, then mark the central vanishing point. The structural lines of your landscape (you might see straight lines in field boundaries or roads) can be drawn with a ruler and must all lead to the vanishing point.

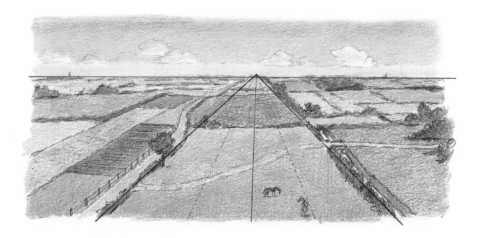

You will find that in landscape drawing the perspective structure is not always immediately obvious as the shapes of nature are not based on straight lines. This view of a path leading through vegetation is more typical of a scene you might draw. Here, the vanishing point is obscured by the trees and there are no straight lines to speak of, however, an understanding of one-point perspective can help you to show how the path recedes into the distance.

Two-point Perspective

This type of perspective usually only comes in use when you are drawing buildings or straight-edged objects and it is unlikely that you will need to employ it in nature drawing. However I've included it here in the event that you want to draw a scene with a building, such as the cottage below. Two-point perspective uses two vanishing points, one at each end of the horizon line.

In this diagram, you can see how the horizontal lines of the cottage recede from the near corner to their respective vanishing points on the far left and right of the landscape. Mostly the vanishing points will be too far out on your horizon line to enable you to plot the converging lines precisely with a ruler. However, if you practise using blocks of buildings using two vanishing points you will soon be able to estimate the converging lines correctly.

Aerial Perspective

This is the name given to perspective as seen through tone and colour. The principle is that if an object is closer to you it will appear more distinct, more textured and with more intense colour than if separated by distance.

Technically, the volume of air, with its accompanying moisture, between you and the object of perception creates a mist of refracted light, and produces the effect that you notice when looking at distant mountains: they always appear more blue than elements of the landscape closer to you. Not only that, their texture is smoothed out and the edges of objects seem less distinct.

So when you produce a landscape, like the two examples here, you can give a greater effect of distance by varying the intensity of the colour and the clarity of the outline.

In the first example, the distant mountains are drawn in blue without very much detail on the surface. As the eye travels towards the foreground, it notices more intense and warmer colour and more distinct detail, as in the fence post and the close-up grass and bushes.

In the second example, a similar effect is produced and this time it is much clearer that the colours of the landscape and building close to the observer are not only more distinct and detailed in texture, but their colours are generally much warmer in tone, using yellows and reds to give a more immediate effect to their position in space. Blue shades, which are cool, tend to recede and red shades, which are warm, tend to advance – or, at least, give the impression of doing so. You can observe this effect for yourself when looking at a large landscape, especially on a damp day. So when you think of perspective, don't forget that colour usage will also enhance the effects of distance and proximity in your picture. Include lots of detail and warmer colours in the foreground, and less detail and cooler colours for the middle and background. Put in the farthest distance features only in blues and greys.

Artist's Tip

The effect of the source of light on the appearance of distance is also key. If your source of light is behind your main features it has the effect of showing them in silhouette, which tends to make them look closer than they are. So if you wish to retain the effect of distance, make sure that the shadowed parts of your objects are shown in as much tonal detail as possible, to ensure that they don't become a silhouette.

The Structure of Landscape

Before you start to draw a larger and more complicated landscape from life, it's advisable to consider how it can be approached schematically. The first point to realize is that in any large open landscape, there's an area of sky with the background immediately below it, then the middle ground and finally the foreground. The horizon line is the edge of the background against the sky.

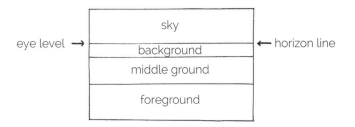

As in my example, parts of the foreground and middle ground will sometimes project into the areas behind, like the large tree in the middle ground that reaches up into the sky.

Sky can be considered as part of background

Background with hardly any tone and minimal texture, very faint and smoother

Middle ground with tone and texture but softer and less intense than the foreground

Foreground with intense tone and contrast and strong textures

In this next version of a landscape we're also aware that the background area is very faint and without detail or much texture – in fact in places it's almost as light as the sky. The middle ground has a little more definition and texture, but still not much detail. The foreground has the greatest definition and the most texture and intensity of detail. This is a result of aerial perspective (see pages 178–9).

Using a Landscape Frame

When you are exploring a location to find a view to draw, a landscape frame can be very useful – not the sort that finished artworks are placed in, but a simple piece of card with a window cut out of it, which corresponds to the shape of the picture that you wish to produce.

Hold up the frame in front of the landscape you are about to draw, in order to decide which part of the view you really want to work on. You always need some way of limiting the parameters, so that the final picture doesn't become too broad for your drawing base.

In the large picture below, there are three outlines superimposed on the general landscape, and you might decide to use one, two or three in your final composition. Each has possibilities but you can choose for yourself the one that is most satisfying to your aesthetic sense.

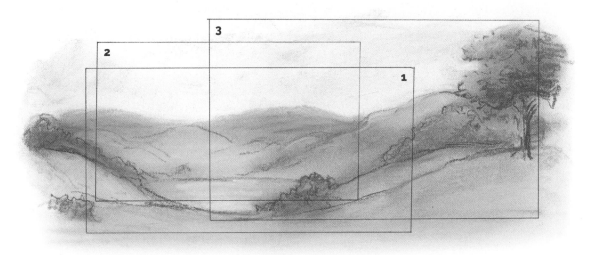

1 The lake in the hills

2 A more concentrated version

3 A view to bring in closer landscape details.

Landscape Variety

Here are a few examples of how you might approach various scenes.

In this view, the landscape takes up almost the whole area of the picture, leaving only a small strip of sky at the top. This is a typical high-horizon view, and eliminates very much interest in the heavens. It is the way that you tend to view a landscape when you are in an elevated position. Because you can see more, you will want to draw more. It may create a mild sense of claustrophobia, but can also lead to a detailed and interesting landscape.

This view is quite the opposite, because the observer occupies a relatively low position and the horizon is therefore also very low. This brings the sky into the picture, and you might find it more interesting when there are some good cloudscapes to draw, rather than on a totally clear day. What this view gives is a great sensation of space.

The next one is an interesting mix of fairly high horizon level and lots of open space in the shape of the sea. The two headlands are the main features of the landscape, but it is the sea that really forms the picture. The noticeable depth in this view has everything to do with the perceived distance between the two headlands. This sort of landscape also gives you a chance to work on the representation of water.

This landscape is enclosed by the grouping of trees around a stretch of water. The viewpoint is from beneath the trees on the bank. The other trees across the small inlet obscure any horizon line. This composition is almost a vignette because of the frame created by the closest trees.

This is a classic case of the path or roadway pulling the viewer deep into the picture. The fence emphasizes this movement, as does the row of trees alongside the road. They naturally draw attention to the little group of cottages at the end of the path. This is a very popular device used by landscapes artist to encourage viewers to engage with the scene.

Exploring a Location

To show that you do not have to travel vast distances to gain plenty of good landscape experience, the next drawings were made within a few hundred yards of the same location, situated within a small area of the county of Surrey, England.

The first landscape view is full of trees and fields that recede towards the misty hills on the horizon. Notice how high the horizon line is, because of the elevated vantage point from which the drawing is done.

The next picture is similar in concept but quite different in texture and depth. The fact that the view is directly down a fairly steep hill helps to give something else to the scene.

The next one is still in the same area but now the light has changed. The closer hills, topped with trees, are almost silhouettes against the skyline and you seem to be able to look around a corner of the high ground to other hillsides beyond. This is quite a gentle landscape, but can be interpreted dramatically depending on the time of day. The little groups of buildings, seen in the middle ground, act as focal points.

The last drawing is of a place about one hundred yards from where the previous drawings were done. However, it looks very different due to the inclusion of part of a wire fence situated close to the onlooker, and also due to an alteration in format, from landscape (horizontal) to portrait (vertical). In this picture the sky becomes more important.

Finding a Viewpoint

You must consider the viewpoint from which you will draw your landscape, because it won't necessarily occur to you by happy accident. As we saw on page 182, you can take a landscape frame with you to help decide on a composition.

A high spot is a good choice, where you can get a good overall view. But then you will have to decide which direction to face and how much of the landscape to include. The dotted lines in this diagram indicate the amount of scope that you may have from a high vantage point.

Sometimes you might be seeking a more gentle or intimate landscape. It is a good idea to position yourself beside a road or river, even a ditch, making use of some extended feature that will draw your eye into the picture. In fact, any device which helps the eye to respond to your drawing, by tempting it to explore your composition, is a good thing. So look for a focal point somewhere in the scene before you.

Using Photographs

Although drawing outside is very good practice, when the weather is cold or wet it's not easy to do. At times like these it's useful to take photographs of the scene that you wish to draw and use these to work from. Take several shots of the same scene from slightly different angles; not only does this give you more information, it often helps to revive your memory of a place, which usually means you get a better drawing.

Here are some landscapes that I drew up for a set of paintings. I took two or three photographs of lakes in parkland on the outskirts of London and as it was winter, and rather cold and wet, I was glad to be able to do this instead of sitting down with an easel and drawing from life.

As you can see, I put the pictures together to form the basis for my drawing, melding the two scenes so that they became one continuous panorama of parkland that gave me more space to play with in the final picture. This was not difficult as the shots I had taken were close together.

Then I went off to the towpath alongside the River Thames near Hampton Court and took two more photographs of the river and the bank close by. In order to get the two pictures to join together I had to draw a bit of the towpath from memory, but that wasn't a problem. The joining of the two pictures made quite a strong composition.

Next I travelled further afield to a part of Surrey where there's a nice stretch of river with an old ruined church nearby. This time I took four shots with the camera and placed them together to form my landscape. This was easily done as there was plenty of information in the photographs and the landscape wasn't very complicated.

The final drawing came from one photograph only, of a wildlife sanctuary on the south coast, where I found a vast growth of teasels along the edge of a path, with a pebble beach landscape in the background. So as you can see, if the situation isn't very good for outdoor drawing you can always use your own photographs as sketchbook information and then draw the final result in the comfort of your home.

A Landscape Project in Steps

Over the next few pages I have shown the stages of a landscape composition, from deciding on a location, to making initial sketches and then working up a final scene. Follow my example or, better still, find your own location and apply the same process.

Choose a location

The first step towards drawing a landscape is deciding on a location. Sometimes this is easy, because you happen to be in a place of great natural beauty and you have your sketchbook – the decision is made for you. However, often the reverse is true; you feel like drawing a landscape but don't have a particular one in mind. So how do you go about setting up a scene?

For this exercise, my first intention was to see how I could work up various sketches that I had done in France and Italy into a more considered composition. I began by drawing up a view of Claude Monet's famous garden at Giverny, in northern France, but finally decided that I wanted something a little less tamed.

So then I looked at some sketches from Italy and worked up a view across a river, with trees in the foreground. However, I eventually felt that I wanted to start afresh with a landscape to draw from real life, so I put away my previous sketches and went out to beautiful Richmond Park, near my home.

This area is of great interest to me because of the variety in its landscape, with lakes, streams, hills and, most notably, magnificent trees. Although it's not wild countryside, it does have a breadth and range that lends itself to exploitation by the landscape artist.

Sketching on location

I went on a long walk with my sketchbook, stopping every now and then to draw what I saw in front of me. The first pause was to draw this view of one of the lakes seen through some large trees. As it was winter there wasn't much foliage, but the bare branches of the taller trees were very attractive things to draw.

Then I moved on to a more open area where a hillside swept up to some woods in the distance. I quickly made a sketch of this and then noticed a large tree that had fallen and was gently rotting away. I made a drawing of this from one side and then moved nearer and around to the other side to make a more detailed drawing – a great thing to use in the foreground of any landscape.

I then drew another glimpse of the lake from a distance, without any trees in front of it. This might come in handy for a background feature. So as you can see, I was beginning to compose a possible landscape picture already, without finalizing my decision yet.

I noticed in the distance a small group of the deer that live in this park and sketched them. It wasn't possible to get very close to them, but they could well be a focal point in a final picture.

I then moved down the hill towards a stream, drawing an attractive tree on the way and then part of a reflection in the stream. I didn't take this very far, because I was realizing that I had now decided what and where I was going to draw.

On top of a hill I drew another log, a man resting on the ground, and a wooden bench. Nearby was a marvellous old dead tree-trunk, split and twisted, making a beautiful sculptural shape, that might be a feature for a foreground.

Step 1

My proposed landscape was to be a view up a hillside, with the large dying tree trunk lying across the path in the foreground. I also thought a couple of deer could appear somewhere in the picture – that is to say, my landscape would be a composite of several views. I made a rough sketch to see how it might look.

Step 2

Feeling that it would work well, I proceeded to draw it up in line only, at which point I could sort out any difficulties of composition and drawing.

Step 3

Once I had made all the corrections I needed to I could now begin to put in the texture and tone to give the picture more body. At this stage I kept the tone even and at its lightest, just in case I needed to change anything.

Step 4

Then came the final push to build up the depth and feeling of space that I wanted to see in the drawing. The deer almost disappear on the hillside, but they do work as a muted focal point in the composition. The path going up the hill helps to draw the eye into the picture and the undulating horizon of the hillside draws the eye around the picture to the dead tree standing on the left.

A Landscape in Watercolour

The medium of watercolour is time-honoured and beloved of many landscape artists, largely because it enables the right effect to be created quickly and easily. It also allows you to cover large areas quickly and brings a nice organic feel to the creative process.

If you are going to tackle a landscape in watercolours, ensure you use watercolour paper or board, the thicker the better. A watercolour sketchbook is well worth taking on expeditions. Ideally you will have two pots for water; one to wash the brush and one to use as fresh liquid for a new colour.

Step 1

First, you need studies of trees to get some idea of what you want your landscape to look like. Here (right) I have made studies of groups of trees and bushes and also a staked wire fence (below). These two elements will both appear in my scene.

Step 2

What I really need is an impressive tree that could be an item by itself. So having found one and made a sketch (right) and a more detailed study (below), I can now assess how to compose my picture.

Artist's Tip

A good way of getting your colours to flow easily in watercolour is to wet the whole area of the paper before you start. This allows you to flood on colours quite easily without leaving any edges or stains in the middle of your wash. Be sure to let it dry fully before you start putting in the more detailed shapes.

Step 3

A quick design gives me an idea of how I shall allow
the eye to be led up to the main tree by the line of the
fence. This helps to give depth in the picture and acts
as a natural indicator to the big tree.

Step 4

Now I can go ahead and produce my scene, giving it a summery look with a blue sky, and making sure the dry, yellow grasses play their part in bringing the attention to the main tree. All the other trees should be much more distant or otherwise insignificant.

Different Media and Effects

Here we consider the variety of techniques you can employ in your landscapes, from brush and wash to mixed media.

In these two brush and wash landscapes, a similar technique has been used to achieve very different effects. In the image opposite an open, spreading landscape is laid out beneath a cloudy sky that takes up two-thirds of the composition. The effect is one of freedom and space. In the landscape below, the sky is notably absent and the scene is set beneath the tree canopy; the mood is one of an ancient, mysterious and darkly shaded woodland.

Next up is a small view along the River Thames, done in mixed media.

First I sketched the outline of the whole scene lightly in pencil and then proceeded to work from the top downwards. All the area above the foreground wall was done with brush and wash, with a few pen and ink marks to indicate the boats gathered by the side of the river. I carefully built up a texture in pencil over the vegetation growing over the wall, and put in some similar marks to indicate the brickwork on the wall and grass on the lawn.

Then I covered the area of the wall and its shadow on the grass using a watercolour wash, making the shadow slightly darker than the wall.

Finally I scrawled in the wall vegetation with a charcoal pencil in order to give it a coarser texture than that of all the other vegetation, smudging it slightly with my thumb.

A Landscape in Coloured Pens

This is a drawing I made in Waterperry Gardens in Oxfordshire, England, using fine-liner pens and felt-tip pens. You can achieve a great intensity of colour and varied textural effects with coloured inks.

Step 1

I started by mapping out the trees and gardens with fine ink lines in green and grey. I used grey to indicate the cloud masses in the sky and green for all the vegetation.

Step 2

Then I put in some larger areas of colour with various felt-tip pens. Using a wide-nibbed felt-tip pen, I added the greyer, shadowed areas of the cumulus clouds. For the grass and vegetation I used a range of colours, layering yellow and light green pen for the grass and lighter foliage. For the darkest areas, I added a touch of purple to dark green to denote deep shadow. I kept the marks sketchy, concentrating on the overall effect rather than precise detail.

Step 3

Having built up the basic shapes and colour areas with felt-tips, I then began to use the fine-liner pens vigorously across the surface. In the sky, I used light horizontal lines for the blue areas and dotted grey for the cloud shadows, leaving the cloud tops white to show the overall formation. On the vegetation and grassland I used a combination of brown, purple, green, red and yellow pens. There were several clumps of flowering shrub in reds and pinks.

The scribble marks I put over some trees convey the effect of thick leafy masses. As you can see you can get a reasonable look of space and vegetation even with these rather less subtle mediums.

Chapter Seven

LANDSCAPE COMPOSITION

This section is all about developing your landscapes further by getting to grips with composition and style. We shall look at various examples of different landscapes, both by myself and after master artists, analysing their composition and stylistic approach.

There are many ways of approaching a landscape, and your own particular view is part of the interest that your drawing will create. A very high eye level or a dramatization of one part of the scene are both valid approaches for an interesting composition. Expanses of calm or turbulent water, large trees and stunning rock formations all bring extra power to your drawing, so make the most of any unusual landscape you come across – but don't feel deterred by more mundane terrain, as the way you handle it can equally catch the viewer's eye.

You will spend more time on a landscape than on any of the other subjects in this book because the sheer scale of a location demands more work and effort. However, when you have finished one you will find it extremely rewarding to have a record of where you have been. There is also something in the human soul that responds to scenes of the natural world; it's no accident that most pictures you see on living-room walls tend to be landscapes of some sort.

Exploring Landscape Compositions

The never-ending interest of drawing landscapes is that there's such a variety of forms, textures and compositions encompassed by the genre. While we all have a particular type of landscape that calls to us the most, it's always possible to find a scene that sparks off a drawing. Over the next pages we'll look at various landscape compositions, some after master artists and some my own.

Our first example is of a large tree that dominates the foreground and in fact the whole picture. The sun is rising behind it so bright patches of light can be seen through its very dark silhouette. The fact that this tree stretches from the top to the bottom of the picture and takes up almost half of the composition means that the rest of the landscape is subordinate to it. Indeed, the picture appears to be mostly background – though the expanse of the field behind the tree is middle ground, it's not very obvious. The row of trees in the background is not much more detailed than the sky, and here the clouds play a big part in the composition. The complexity of this composition is subtle and depends on your ability to draw the clouds interestingly enough to contrast with the dominant tree.

The next picture is of a landscape in which the main feature is again trees, but this time a group of them in the middle ground. A curving path extends from the forefront of the composition and swings around behind the trees, helping to pull the viewer's eye into the picture towards the main feature. Behind that is a row of low hills covered in vegetation with a bank of bushes in the near foreground.

The third scene is of a mountainous landscape with rows of rocky peaks in the background, similar terrain in the middle ground and scrub-covered lumps of rock in the foreground. The great difficulty in a scene like this is to show the difference in distance between the nearest outcrops and the far mountains. If you're lucky there'll be some light mist between the further ranges and the middle ground outcrops, as in this picture; if not, rendering the texture and detail well-defined in the foreground and lessening towards the background is the best way. Notice how in this example the view has been selected so the nearest mountains are shown to the sides of the picture, and the furthest mountains are most prominent in the centre of the composition.

Here's a composition rather like the first example on page 218, in which a very large tree in the foreground tends to dominate the scene. However, unlike the first picture, the lines of the ploughed landscape pull the eye into the scene and lead it into the background hills and woods. The structure of the main tree is very evident here and becomes the most interesting part of the drawing.

The next scene is primarily about the water in the foreground and how it reflects the rest of the scenery in the surface. The middle ground is mostly trees with a gap opening up the background to one side. As the lake takes up half of the whole composition it's quite important in the drawing and the reflections need to look convincing.

These two compositions are after the Viennese painter Gustav Klimt (1862–1918), who specialized in decorative effects. They complement each other, the first having most of the scene made up of the grassy foreground and the other picture composed mainly of the massed leaves of the trees. Klimt tended to reduce the depth of his paintings to flatter, more abstract areas of texture, and in the first example the large area of grass is given a little depth only by the spaced silver birch trees and the mass of dark trees in the background.

Here the mass of the background trees becomes the main area of the composition, while the foreground and middle ground are squashed into a very small area at the bottom. These effects give quite a dramatic quality to the landscapes, and the texture of the grass and leaves in both is treated in a very decorative way.

In the landscape below the main theme is the avenue of trees along the road, taking the attention of the viewer into the centre of the picture and disappearing into the dark clouds covering the lower parts of the sky. In this picture the stormy sky in the background is in fact the element that is brought to your attention by means of the avenue leading into the distance.

On the left is a version of a Claude Monet (1840–1926) painting of a beach, from which I have removed all the people to show how the landscape itself takes your attention from the foreground sweeping away around the bay to the distant horizon of the sea. The boats drawn up on the shore in the immediate foreground grab the attention first and as the coast leads the eye around we see the middle-ground dinghy and then, in the far distance, what appear to be more sails out at sea. The sky in this composition takes up half the space and is important, with its dappled cloudscape making a contrast to the lower half.

The two landscapes shown on these pages both have a high vantage point and use a similar colour palette in coloured pencils, but portray very different types of terrain. In the first, vegetation sweeps across undulating grasslands in a mixture of trees and bushes. It looks mainly a pleasant, open space of small fields and patches of woodland. There is not much drama in this landscape but it nevertheless shows an attractive view.

The second example, set in a highland region, shows a more varied, striking landscape. There is a lake in the centre, which dramatically breaks the formation of the surrounding wooded hills. The dark wooded areas show in great contrast to the areas of open, tilled land. Close to our viewpoint is a gash of open, dug-up soil, which has a ruddy glow. In the distance we can see blue-grey mountain masses cutting into the skyline. Even the clouds look heavier than in the previous picture. This a dramatic landscape with a central feature of water.

In this scene the river is pulling the eye towards the distant scenery, but the dramatic cloudy sky above seems to stretch our attention sideways to consider the breadth of the space. This sky with its reflection in the river surface is quite effective in opening up the space in the scene. The arrows in the diagram on the right show the direction the eye takes when reading the image.

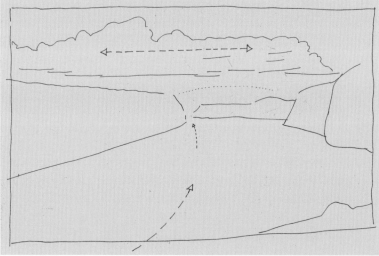

The next scene, of the dramatic coast in Dorset, England, is more complex. The centre of the composition is the circular inlet of the sea in the rocky cliff face. All the lower parts of the picture seem to indicate the direction towards this centre. The cliffs immediately above the pool also move the eye down to the water. The sky above and the slanting line of the cliff top with its row of trees and the distant downland all move the attention towards the centre line of the cliff face which dips down towards the edge of the pool.

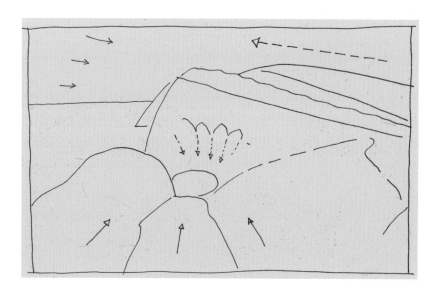

This drawing of the English Lake District has a similar effect to the coastal scene on the previous page in that the rocky edges of the lake all seem to draw our attention towards the water. The water appears to swing around the edge of the rocks, while the activity of the clouds swirls around to bring the eye back to the centre of the scene.

A lakeside scene after Claude Lorrain (1602–82) is slightly more complex, as you would expect from this master of landscape. The big tree on the left hems in our vision, while the foreground pulls our attention towards the area of the water. The outline of the distant landscape and the large trees sweeping down to the river on the right also concentrate the eye on the water. However, the key element is the strong vertical tower built on the riverbank which holds our attention for contemplation. This is the real centre of the piece and everything else tends to pull our attention towards it or across it.

Figures in the Landscape

The next three drawings give some idea as to the potential of figures and man-made objects in a landscape and how they affect the composition.

The first example, after *Bright Summer* (1892) by the Royal Academician Marcus Stone (1840–1921), is of a garden with trees and a fairly low horizon. The picture is almost in two halves except for the strong lines that cut into the horizon. The diagonal from the tops of the trees on the left uses the horizon as a base and divides the upper half of the picture. The seated figure in the lower half links up with the other tree line on the right of the picture and draws the viewer's attention to the activity of the young woman seated there. This helps to create a space across the middle of the composition.

John George Naish (1824–1905) sets his scene behind the sea wall of a small harbour in the Channel Islands, *Le Creux Harbour, Sark* (1858). Cutting out any deep sense of landscape are the rocky cliffs and then to the left is a large wall, casting a shadow across the water. Near the foreground some boats are moored, and just about to disappear behind the harbour wall is another boat with two men in it. So although we are aware of how spacious the harbour is, it is carefully circumscribed by the wall and the farther rocks.

The next example is a picture of Pegwell Bay by William Dyce (1806–64), a Victorian artist. Here the composition is a very simple halfway horizon with a range of chalk cliffs jutting into it. All the action in the picture is in the lower half, with various areas of rock and sand on which people are gathering shells and so forth. Most of the significant action is in the immediate foreground, though small figures are dotted across the middle ground, emphasizing the scale of the scene. The ladies in their crinolines make pleasing large simple shapes.

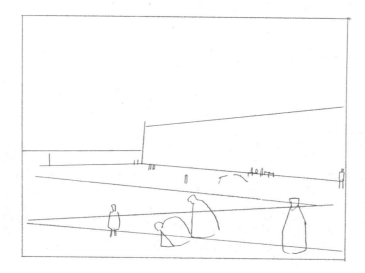

Portrait Format

When it comes to drawing landscapes the usual tendency is to think in terms of a wide horizontal shape, which is indeed known as landscape format. However, a vertical shape (portrait format) can sometimes be an interesting variation that may suit your subject better. Here are three versions of portrait-format pictures that show how this way of selecting your scene can be useful.

The first scene is of a narrow walkway near Florence, Italy, which shows tall trees either side of a walled road. The whole interest of the picture is the perspective effect of the tunnel through the encroaching walls and trees. If you were standing in this spot it would be obvious that a portrait format is the way to draw the scene.

The next drawing is a much more selective view, because the natural way to portray an open beach scene without much in the way of foreground features is to show it in a wide horizontal format. Here, with the sides of the picture pulled in, the magnificent cloud is the main feature; the sea and beach have been reduced to the minimum so as not to distract from the view of the sky. This sort of landscape could correctly be described as a skyscape instead.

This scene was drawn very late in the day when the low sun was making silhouettes of the boats and trees. It's more a picture of the sun and its effect on the misty sky and the water rather than of the lake itself, so the portrait format was used to act as a window that selects the sun and its reflection. The passing boat in the centre of the scene is a bonus, only made possible by using photographs for information; a moment such as this doesn't allow time for detailed sketching.

A Panoramic View

This picture of downland scenery to the south of London was drawn in the 18th century by George Lambert (1700–65). He chose a wide format to include as much of the panorama as possible, positioning himself well back from the hill – he even shows another artist in front of him drawing the scene.

Tackling a panorama

When you feel ready to have a go at a complex large-scale picture such as this you will need to set it up carefully. You will obviously have to choose a day when the weather is going to be in your favour, and then you will have to find a spot to draw from that makes it easier for you to encompass the whole scene. It's a time-consuming subject, too, so you'll have to allot a good part of the day to your drawing, or else return several times in order to complete the picture. A good series of photographs will help to add extra information for completing the piece when you get it home.

Working on a piece this large is always a challenge, but if you have the courage to try it out you will probably learn a good deal about landscape drawing in quite a short time. If the view is local to you, visiting it repeatedly beforehand will tell you a lot about the times of day the light is most attractive and the best spots to place yourself. It will also help you to regard the scene as a familiar one, making the moment you arrive with your paper and pencils less daunting.

Using Colour

The choice of medium can sometimes be particularly appropriate to the type of landscape you are working on. 'The medium is the message,' said Marshall McLuhan in the 1960s and, in drawing, this is no exception. Here are two landscapes that give quite different effects, and the mediums seem particularly suited to the type of scene being shown. One seems to be glowing with energy and fiery, while the other is cool and gentle in effect.

This first example is after the antique Chinese landscape from *c.* 1685 by K'un Ts'an, with melting mountain ranges and sketchy trees. To create this version I first used sepia ink and then green ink, carefully portraying the intricate details of the rocky hills and twisted trees. After this, keeping very subdued like the original, came softly applied layers of coloured pencil, using the edge of a well-sharpened point in violet, brown, green and blue.

The second example shows a pastel version of one of Claude Monet's Haystack paintings (a series of at least 25 variations), which glows with golden light and gives the impression of the haystack almost burning up. The original was done with oil paints, but can be effectively imitated by pastel in the same way as Monet worked his paint. These impressionistic strokes of brilliant colour allow you to show the dazzling effects of hot sun when it is low in the sky.

William Turner's watercolour painting of *Okehampton Castle* (1814) shows us how he fitted his colour scheme to suit a particular landscape. The castle appears on top of a rocky hill covered in trees and bushes, dominating the surrounding rocky landscape by the river Okement. Close to our viewpoint are lots of jumbled rocks and sawn-off tree trunks. The two figures in the middle ground give some idea of the size of the surrounding landscape. The two slender trees to the right of the composition contrast with the rocky hills on the left. The colours are mostly brown and tan, giving a good idea of the rugged quality of this terrain. The areas of green help to accentuate this effect and draw the eye up to the castle on its green summit.

To make this moonlit landscape in watercolour I had to take a different approach to adding colour. In the early evening there was not enough light to paint it from life or to take a reasonable photograph, so I made drawings and sketches with notes to describe the colours and tones. Later I made this painting to convey the drama, with dark trees and fields glowing in the evening light. I started with the lightest colours, letting these dry before adding the darkest blues and greens of the trees and sky. This fairly nondescript landscape is given mystery and drama by the unusual light and colours.

Drama and Expression

Many natural landscapes are inherently dramatic, especially those in mountainous areas or by sheer cliffs. In the following examples we'll explore how artists have used strong tonal contrasts, angled viewpoints and expressive marks to capture the sense of awe they feel before the natural world.

First, a work by Richard Wilson (1714–82), showing the top of Cader Idris in Wales. The design focuses on the large triangle of the peak, dominating the calm waters of the lake. Because of the dramatic view, the tones are important as they give power to the dark peak silhouetted against the sky. The inclusion of a few small figures gives a sense of scale in this wild, mountainous landscape.

The Romantic artists of the 19th century vied with each other to produce dramatic landscapes of towering crags and toppling mountains. *Gordale Scar* by James Ward (1769–1859) belongs to this great tradition, its effect so powerful as to almost overwhelm the first-time viewer. Many other painters at this time in Europe and America were producing works of staggering size and powerful dramatic effect, such as John 'Mad' Martin (1789–1854), Caspar David Friedrich (1774–1840), Frederic Edwin Church (1826–1900) and Albert Bierstadt (1830–1902).

The next picture, after *Sikyon with Corinth* by the German artist, Carl Rottmann (1797–1850), builds drama into the landscape by means of the harsh rocky surfaces revealed by the raking sunlight. Notice how the artist has hidden most of the detail beneath the dark shadows that stretch over the scene. The block-like way he has shown the rugged terrain works wonderfully to convince us that this is a remorseless, desert-like landscape.

In *View from Mount Holyoke* after Thomas Cole (1801–48), we see the landscape from on high and it appears almost like a map below us. Half of the view is obscured by an enormous rainstorm, sweeping across the left-hand side of the picture. With just a little detail added to the stunted tree in the foreground, the plain is laid out below us with the enormous river winding around it.

This panorama of Dartmoor, in Devon, is after the Victorian artist John William Inchbold (1830–88). With this type of landscape you need to find a place that gives you key features to help frame the composition, which Inchbold has done well with the large rock on the left and the deep ravine on the right. The sweep of the sky is kept to about one-quarter of the whole area of the picture, so that it doesn't distract from the rugged scenery. Overall accuracy is not the most important part of a drawing such as this – capturing the atmosphere of the place comes first.

Post-Impressionist artists in the late 19th century used innovative styles and techniques to express their individual view of the landscape. *Mont Sainte-Victoire* after Paul Cézanne (1839–1906) has considerable drama, mainly thanks to his way of structuring the solid shapes of the land and the clouds in the sky. The textural effect of his marks on the canvas makes this a very powerful, brooding image.

The sky plays a very dramatic role in this example of a cornfield with cypress trees after Vincent van Gogh (1853–90). The picture is characterized by strange, swirling marks for the sky, trees and fields. The feeling of movement in the air is potently expressed by the cloud shapes, which, like the plants, are reminiscent of tongues of fire. Somehow the shared swirling characteristic seems to harmonize the elements, as well as expressing the artist's inner turmoil. The original painting was produced not very long before Van Gogh killed himself.

The Seven Sisters

For the final drawing in this book, I've chosen a scene that brings together many elements we've looked at so far. These dramatic white chalk cliffs in southern England are known as the Seven Sisters. The view encompasses the sea, an area of beach and the sky with scudding clouds, as well as vegetation and grasslands.

Step 1

Such a large view as this may seem daunting as there is so much to fit on to the paper. The trick is to break it down, identifying areas of path, grass, sea, beach and cliffs. Make a very rough sketch to indicate these areas.

Step 2

This is the most important stage of your drawing. Firm up your initial sketch, taking particular care over the shapes of the cliffs as these are very distinctive. The straight angles of your composition are formed by the sea on the right, which is a clear horizontal, and the small buildings in the centre. The fence on the left and the path on the right, although not so clear-cut, will play their part in the composition, leading the eye into the centre of the picture and on to the cliffs beyond.

Step 3

Once you are happy with the overall structure of your picture, start to add colour in light tones. I have used coloured pencils, but you may prefer another medium. Spend some time identifying the areas of highlight and variation in colour across the landscape. On the downs on the left-hand side, the grass is criss-crossed by light-coloured paths, where hundreds of people have walked along the cliffs. The colours of the sea will depend on the clouds above, but will always darken to a strong line across the horizon.

Step 4

Finally, strengthen your colours across the image to give it some depth. Add darker greens to deeply shaded areas of vegetation, and overlay your colours where necessary to get the correct tones. For the cliffs, add grey only sparingly to denote the craggier parts, as the subject of your drawing is, after all, the white cliffs.

Index